E-M

In An Instant

60 Ways to Communicate With Style and Impact

E-Mail In An Instant

- Compose Messages That Save Time for Everyone
- Learn to Separate the Trivial From the Important
- Minimize E-Mail Misunderstandings

Karen Leland and Keith Bailey

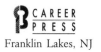

CAREER PRESS
Franklin Lakes, NJ

E-MAIL IN AN INSTANT
EDITED BY KARA REYNOLDS
TYPESET BY MICHAEL FITZGIBBON
Cover design by Howard Grossman / 12E Design
Printed in the U.S.A. by Book-mart Press

To order this title, please call toll-free 1-800-CAREER-1 (NJ and Canada: 201-848-0310) to order using VISA or MasterCard, or for further information on books from Career Press.

The Career Press, Inc., 3 Tice Road, PO Box 687,
Franklin Lakes, NJ 07417
www.careerpress.com

Library of Congress Cataloging-in-Publication Data

Bailey, Keith, 1945-
E-mail in an instant : 60 ways to communicate with style and impact / by Keith Bailey and Karen Leland.
p. cm.
Includes Index.
ISBN 978-1-60163-017-9
1. Electronic mail systems. 2. Electronic mail messages. 3. Business communication. I. Leland, Karen. II. Title.

HE7551.B35 2009
808'.066651--dc22

2008045979

To my wife, Deborah. Your support, encouragement, wisdom, and humor are like the wind at my back. Thank you.
—Keith Bailey

To my parents, Norman and Barbara Tiber, for always showing interest and asking to read what I am writing about—regardless of the topic.
—Karen Leland

Acknowledgments

Many thanks to our agent, Matthew Carnicelli, and the folks at Career Press for their support of the In An Instant series. Much gratitude to our clients and all the executives, managers, and front-line staff with whom we have had the privilege of working—in our seminars and speeches—and learning from. Last, but far from least, to our spouses, Deborah and Jon—your ongoing support means everything.

Contents

Introduction **15**

1. Assess Your E-Mail Savvy 17

2. Be Concise and to the Point 20

3. Prioritize Your Paragraphs 22

4. Discover the Secret of Sensory Language 25

5. Mirror Key Words 28

6. Be Formal With Neutral Language 31

7. Make Your E-Mails Action-Packed 33

8. Make Effective Requests 35

9. Use the E.M.A.I.L. Acronym 37

10. Say No With Style 39

11. Engage the Expressive Style 41

12. Step Into the Straight-Shooter Style 44

13. Ease Into the Nice and Easy Style 46

14. Be Part of the Problem-Solving Style 48

15. Start With a Salutation 50

16. Craft a Compelling Subject Line 53

17. Sign Off With Substance 55

18. Go Easy on the CC 58

19. BCC With Caution 60

20. Consider Attachment Options 62

21. Open Attachments With Care 64

22. Shorten Your Sentences 65

23. Vary Your Sentence Length 68

24. Choose Your Sentence Style With Care 70

25. Put the Apostrophe in Its Place 72

26. Consider the Common Comma 74

27. Save Time With Contractions 77

28. Capitalize on Cue 79

29. Use the Trusty Transition 82

30. Master the Most Misspelled Words 83

31. Sharpen Your Spelling 87

32. Don't Get Hung Up on Homophones 89

33. Avoid the 10 Top E-Mail Mistakes 92

34. Get a Grip on the Jargon 96

35. Don't Fan the Flames 99

36. Nix the Negative Filters 102

37. Beware Obscure Emoticons 103

38. Sort Through Spam 106

39. Avoid Phishing Like the Plague 108

40. Beef Up Your E-Mail Security 110

41. Set Up a Responsible Rant 112

42. Keep Cultural Differences in Mind 113

43. Create an E-Mail Policy 116

44. Write an E-Mail Policy 117

45. Brainstorm Possible Problem Causes 120

46. Evaluate Possible Problem Causes 122

47. Brainstorm Possible Problem Solutions 123

48. Evaluate and Agree on the Problem Solution 124

49. Find an E-Mail Marketing Service 126

50. Plan an E-Mail Marketing Newsletter 129

51. Send Out an E-Mail Marketing Newsletter 131

52. Get Good at Instant Messaging 134

53. Study Your IM Shorthand 136

54. E-Mail on a PDA 137

55. Use POP and IMAP 139

56. Know When to Stop 141

57. Don't Use E-Mail 143

58. Manage Your Files 145

59. Set Up Your Filing System 147

60. Zero Out Your Inbox 151

Conclusion 153

Index 155

About the Authors 159

About Sterling Consulting Group 160

Introduction

Read 10 different e-mails, from 10 different people, and you'll more than likely come across a whole slew of writing styles, a wide gap in e-mail etiquette, and a huge variation in tone.

The beauty of e-mail is that it gives you the freedom to be casual and chatty in one communication and formal in another. You'll probably find that your e-mail style changes depending on to whom you are writing (customer, coworker, wife, perspective client), and about what you are writing.

Although there may not be one *best* approach for all e-mail communications, *E-Mail In An Instant* will help you assess the most effective and efficient ways to get your message across with style and impact.

More than 25,000 people have attended our live or online Essential E-Mail courses. In this book we have attempted to distill the key principles and practices we teach into 60 easy-to-use actions. Going beyond basic etiquette, we've looked at e-mail from every angle, including: how to organize your inbox, create and send an e-mail marketing newsletter, express emotion electronically, and win friends and influence people—all with a click of the keyboard.

1

Assess Your E-Mail Savvy

Although e-mail is the most frequently used vehicle for business communication, the finer points of when and how to use it are often overlooked. To test out your e-mail excellence, answer the following multiple-choice questions.

1. Typing an e-mail in all caps:
   a. Is the online equivalent of yelling or screaming.
   b. Makes you look unprofessional.
   c. Puts a strain on the reader's eyes.

Answer: A. E-mail etiquette dictates that all caps equals yelling. Unless the word requires capitalization (as in the case of an acronym or name), avoid this online faux pas.

2. An e-mail should only be CC'd when:
   a. The other person needs to have the information.
   b. The topic is interesting.
   c. It's important.

Answer: A. The unnecessary CCing of e-mails to coworkers, customers, bosses, and vendors has become an epidemic. Only copy people who have a hands-on relationship with the topic (or need to know the content of your message) on an e-mail.

3. The BCC field is most useful for:
   a. Avoiding having to send a second, separate e-mail.
   b. Including someone involved in a situation while protecting his or her privacy.
   c. Sending copies to anyone I want without getting caught.

Answer: B. The BCC is a great way to include one or more people in the loop without making their e-mail addresses known to everyone else on the list.

4. E-mails should be answered:
   a. As soon as possible.
   b. When I get around to it.
   c. Within two days.

Answer: A. Although it would be nice if all e-mails could be responded to within 24 hours, the workload in most offices makes this impossible. If you can answer an e-mail right away and clear it off your list, great. If not, getting an incoming e-mail processed as soon as possible, and hopefully within two days, is the next best solution.

5. E-mail paragraphs should be:
   a. As long as they need to be.
   b. As short as possible.
   c. Irrelevant.

Answer: B. Short paragraphs are easier on the eye and allow readerd to scan the message and find the information they most need to see.

6. If I have several points I want to make in a single e-mail, I should:
   a. Make all the points in one paragraph.
   b. Save all the points until the end of the e-mail and group them together.
   c. Use a list format with bullets or numbers.

Answer: C. Grouping points all together in one paragraph makes them hard to read and increases the chance that they will get lost in the shuffle. To make your points stand apart, use bullets, and list them in logical order.

7. A good subject line:
   a. Contains a greeting.
   b. Up to 75 characters in length.

c. Is specific to the topic and no longer than a sentence.

Answer: C. The more on-topic and on-target you are, the greater the chance the receiver will open your message. The typical subject line will display up to 35 characters.

8. If you need to send a large attachment:
   a. Attach it to your e-mail and send.
   b. Contact the other party first to let him or her know it's coming.
   c. Compress it or break it up into several downloads.

Answer: B and C. Depending on what the other person's system can handle, you may be able to send a great big file with no problem. If bandwidth is an issue, breaking up the file is the nice thing to do.

9. Which information should never be e-mailed?
   a. Credit card numbers.
   b. Social Security numbers.
   c. Phone numbers.

Answer: B. Most online commerce sites have security measures in place to protect you when giving a credit card number on the Internet. But anything else you wouldn't want shared with unknown parties, such as Social Security numbers and bank account numbers, should be kept out of an e-mail.

10. A highly emotional situation should be dealt with by:
    a. A face-to-face conversation.
    b. Telephone.
    c. A detailed and unemotional e-mail.

Answer: A. The most information another person uses to interpret your feelings and attitudes comes from body language. The second greatest amount of information comes from tone of voice. E-mail, which lacks both of these, is the worst choice for discussing emotional or sensitive issues.

2

Be Concise and to the Point

Imagine having a heated conversation with one of your associates, in which you are excitedly explaining your ideas about a lunchtime Jacuzzi party. Your message would probably be conveyed in a torrent of words, ideas tumbling out in random order. Because you are engaged in a dialogue, your conversation partner is not concerned about the words you use, your sentence structure, or the repetitiousness of your vocabulary. But in e-mail, unlike in a real-life conversation, your reader is focused on the words, and nothing more, so your message must be more precise, your sentences shorter, and your ideas presented in a logical order.

An e-mail written the same way the sender speaks is heard to read and easy to ignore. For example:

From: Tanya Hideoff
Subject: Lunchtime Jacuzzi Party
Date: May 17
To: Allison Wonderland

Dear Allison:

I am soooo excited about this idea that I just came up with! I was sitting at my desk staring out the window and chewing on a pencil when I had this flash of brilliance! Why not forego the footlong, dump the deli, say sianara to the sandwich, and sit in hot water at lunch instead of stuffing our faces?

Just think of it. You'd come back to work refreshed and ready to turbo-tap the keyboard to a new level of productivity—plus you'd be losing weight at the same time. Who needs lunch? And anyway, if we got hungry we could always have a protein bar handy. The hot water would be invigorating and relaxing, just what the doctor ordered after a hectic morning of e-mail-writing and phone calls.

The one problem is that there isn't a Jacuzzi anywhere close. The nearest is across town and it would take at least an hour there and back. I am following up with Lisa Mona, in sales, she has one at her house that she says we can use as long as we contribute to the cost of heating the tub. Which won't be a lot. Probably no more than $3 a month for each of us. Her place is relatively close and she said she would provide us with towels as part of the deal. Lisa can be a bit temperamental, so I'd like to find an alternative, just in case she flakes out at the last minute.

Would you be willing to talk to people in your department to see if you can come up with alternatives? I think Adam Sapple has one at his place but I'm not sure.

Okay, let me know what you think. I can't wait to get started!

Best,
Tanya

P.S. Lisa's tub can hold up to six people but I want to be really selective about who we invite to our lunchtime lounging session. ;-)

Phew! Did you make it through to the end? Tanya's e-mail is way too chatty and ridiculously long. If Allison is busy (and who isn't?), there's a good chance that she will stop reading long before the end. If Tanya trimmed the fat on this e-mail, she could still convey her ideas, but in a way that keeps the reader interested. For example:

From: Tanya Hideoff
Subject: Lunchtime Jacuzzi Party
Date: May 17
To: Allison Wonderland

Dear Allison:

I just came up with a great idea: spending lunchtime in a Jacuzzi! It would be relaxing and refreshing, and would rejuvenate us for work in the afternoon. The closest tub belongs to Lisa Mona, in sales; she has one at her house that she says we can use if we pay something toward the electric bill.

Let me know if you are interested.

Best,
Tanya

3

Prioritize Your Paragraphs

Walking into work can occasionally feel like stepping inside a blender; the day becomes a blur of activity, with too much to do and too little time in which to do it. It's hardly surprising that many people save time by only reading the first few sentences of an e-mail.

If the first paragraph doesn't catch their attention, then it's a quick flick of the erase button and on to the next message. To make sure your message gets read—amid the torrent of daily e-mails—think about what paragraph contains the most meaningful information, and place it at the top, with the least important paragraph being the last.

Exercise

Read through the following e-mail and prioritize each paragraph by writing its position number in the space provided. (Position #1 = first paragraph, position #2 = second paragraph, and so on.)

Subject: Upcoming Steering Committee Meeting
From: Willy Ketchum
Date: August 8
To: All Department Heads

Dear Steering Committee Members:

Position Number ____

As many of you remarked, the last meeting was very unorganized, with an outcome that was disappointing after discussions lasting for more than two hours.The meeting started 15 minutes late, and then ran over by 40 minutes. As the organizer, I owe everyone a big apology, and I am working dilligently to make the next meeting better.

Position Number ____

The headlines from the last meeting that I have gathered together, from your comments and my own memory, are as follows: (1) New delivery trucks should all leave a small carbon footprint. (2) Our logo should be on the sides, back, and top of the trucks so it can be seen by passing air traffic. (3) They should all be equipped with satellite navigation units.

Position Number ____

For the next meeting I have invited Mr. Collins, from dispatch, to come and talk to us about how the delivery process works and in what ways the trucks are to be used. This way we can all be on the same page.

Position Number ____

The next meeting is on Tuesday, August 21, at 10 a.m. To make the time work for Mr. Collins, we will be meeting at the Jones Road Warehouse. I suggest we carpool. Please contact me if you need a ride.

Sincerely,
Willy Ketchum

Answers and Rationale

Position 1: *The next meeting is on Tuesday, August 21, at 10 a.m. To make the time work for Mr. Collins, we will be meeting at the Jones Road Warehouse. I suggest we carpool. Please contact me if you need a ride.*

This paragraph contains the vital information for the next meeting. By putting it first you insure that every recipient, no matter how little of the e-mail they might read, has what they need for the next meeting.

Position 2: *The headlines from the last meeting that I have gathered together, from your comments and my own memory, are as follows: (1) New delivery trucks should all leave a small carbon footprint. (2) Our logo should be on the sides, back, and top of the trucks so it can be seen by passing air traffic. (3) They should all be equipped with satellite navigation units.*

Once everyone has the information about where and when, this paragraph serves to support the next meeting by reminding readers of the key topics from the last meeting.

Position 3: *For the next meeting I have invited Mr. Collins, from dispatch, to come and talk to us about how the delivery process works and in what ways the trucks are to be used. This way we can all be on the same page.*

Although this is useful information, it doesn't matter if it is never read because it can easily be announced to the attendees once they are in the meeting.

Position 4: *As many of you remarked, the last meeting was very unorganized, with an outcome that was disappointing after discussions lasting for more than two hours.The meeting started 15 minutes late and then ran over by 40 minutes. As the organizer, I owe everyone a big apology, and I am working diligently to make the next meeting better.*

Acknowledging the mess-up at the last meeting is commendable, but, because it has no direct impact on the next meeting, putting it as the first paragraph uses up space for more pertinent information.

4

Discover the Secret of Sensory Language

If you read through a few of the e-mails you have recently received, you will more than likely notice that the writer's overall style contains language that relates to one of three primary senses:

- Auditory: "The meeting sounds like a good idea to me."
- Visual: "I see why we need a meeting."
- Feeling: "I feel strongly that a meeting is in order."

When it comes to making a "connection" with the people to whom you reach out and respond via e-mail, it's easier to establish rapport when you know the secret of using sensory language. The trick, when replying to an e-mail, is to find what specific type of words the writer uses more than any other. You can do this by observing whether the writer's language is more auditory-, visual-, or feeling-oriented. For example:

- If a more visual writer is interested in finding out about your products or services, he or she might write: "I look forward to getting a clearer idea about the services you offer."
- A more auditory-oriented writer might put it this way: "I'd like to talk with you by phone about the products you offer and hear exactly how you think they might help my company."
- Someone with a "feeling" style of writing might say: "I'd like to get a better feel for what you provide, and a handle on your services."

After you've quickly reviewed the e-mail and uncovered the writer's preferred sensory style, you can respond in kind by using sensory words that are consistent with the writer's. Without realizing why, the person on the other end of your e-mail messages will feel more connected and better understood because of the rapport-building quality of your message. Following is a chart that shows some common words and phrases for each sensory style. In time, you can add your own examples.

4

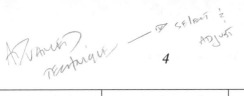

Visual	Auditory	Feeling
Perspective	Quiet	Touch
Picture	Listen	Smooth
Look	Noise	Grasp
Vague	Say	Handle
Focus	Talk	Firm
Clear	Tone	Warm
Hazy	Harmony	Pressure
Illuminate	Sounds	Cold
Scan	Orchestrate	Hard
Vision	Dissonance	Fragmented
Bright	Clicked	Feel
Lighten up	Resonates	Solid
Blank	Loud	Lighter
Dark	Rings a bell	Getting to
Imagine	Sounds like	Comfortable
Clarify	On that note	Moving along
Color	Clear as a bell	Rough
Playful	Hear	Relaxed
Pale	Static	
Dull	Music	
See	Trickle	
Black and white		
Crystallize		

Exercise

Read through the following e-mails and write a response to each one using the appropriate sensory language that will help the writer feel more connected and understood. You may want to refer to the chart to see what words/phrases you can use in your response.

I feel really upset that the cat chow was delivered a week late. It stresses me to worry about Buffy getting her nutritional needs met.

Your response: ______________________________

I see from glancing at the mail today that Buffy's cat chow has still not arrived. I will be looking for it over the next few days. Please take care of this right way.

Your response: ______________________________

If I sound upset in this e-mail, let me explain, Buffy is very important to me and I am still waiting for her cat chow; it was supposed to be here yesterday.

Your response: ______________________________

5

Mirror Key Words

Face-to-face conversations provide you with countless clues about the person with whom you are talking. For example, a colleague's tone of voice can let you know that his or her remarks were tongue-in-cheek and not to be taken seriously, or, a customer's facial expression can make it crystal clear that, though he or she seems calm on the outside, the customer is boiling mad underneath. Being the sensitive individual you are, once you catch wind of the other person's mood or attitude, you respond in a way that creates rapport—right?

Finding these clues with e-mail messages is like looking for a needle in a haystack, and creating rapport, a champion challenge. One way to do it is to pay close attention to the specific, key words the writer uses and lightly sprinkle them throughout your response. Seeing their key words come back at them in the response will help readers feel more rapport with and connection to the writer.

Imagine receiving this e-mail message from a new client:

From: April Showers
Subject: Broken Television
Date: March 5
To: Customer Service

Hello,

I purchased a flat-screen television made by your company three weeks ago, and am very upset by the fact that the picture has all of a sudden turned upside-down. The set was professionally installed and has been working perfectly until the flip-flop happened. I have to stand on my head to watch the late show! As you can visualize, this is only a short-term solution.

The set is still under warranty, and I would like one of your tech sharpshooters to come over and sort things out as soon as possible so that I can resume a normal siting position when viewing my shows.

Thank you,
April Showers

As you read through this e-mail message, see if you can pick out the key words and phrases the writer is using to convey her unique feelings, mood, attitude, and point of view. List them in the spaces following.

Answers

In this message the key words are:

- all of a sudden
- set

- flip-flop
- late show
- visualize
- sharpshooters

To create rapport, when crafting your reply, be sure to mirror some or all of the key words you have identified. For example:

Subject: Broken Television
From: Customer Service
Date: March 6
To: April Showers

Dear Ms. Showers,

Thank you for your letter. I apologize for the problems you are having with the picture flip-flopping on your set. Unfortunately, we do not have technicians in the field; all our repair work is done by sharpshooters at our repair center.

Your set is under warranty, so I can arrange for it to be picked up for repair. Hopefully you will be watching the late show again within the week.

Please let me know a date when we can pick up the set.

Sincerely,
Reggie R.
Customer Service

Exercise

Read through the following message and underline the key words.

5–6

From: Art Maker
Subject: Insurance policy question
Date: Feb 9
To: Bob Roberts, Agent

Dear Bob:

I need to revise my homeowner's policy that I carry with you. I want to append a new camera and some jewelry.

Could you shoot me the required forms so that I can get these articles on the policy ASAP? Thanks.

Art

Answers: carry, append, shoot, required, articles.

6

Be Formal With Neutral Language

Much of the language used in business is non-sensory, or neutral. In other words, it does not provide any clue as to which type of sensory modality (visual, auditory, or feeling) the writer prefers. For example, a writer with a preference for visual words may say, "I can <u>see</u> what you mean." An auditory response would be, "I <u>hear</u> what you are saying." And so on. If you want to send an e-mail that has a high degree of formality, and sounds more official or legal, then use neutral language. Some of the most common neutral words used in business include:

* COMMON NEUTRAL WORDS

Abstract	Believe	Cogent	Connote
Comprehend	Conceptualize	Consider	Deduce
Denote	Formalize	Idea	Indicate
Induce	Involve	Know	Learn
Make	Occurs	Organize	Reason
Recall	Recognize	Remember	Suppose
Seems	Think	Understand	

Exercise

Consider the following facts and take a stab at crafting an e-mail in the space following, using only neutral language.

- Jim Smith ordered a dozen daiquiri-flavored doughnuts to be mailed overnight from your Website, *www.deliciousdoughnutsareus.com*.
- The doughnuts arrived on time, but were margarita-flavored, not daiquiri.
- Jim Smith is upset and has written an e-mail asking what happened.
- Your company is willing to ship the correct order overnight at no charge.

____

____

How did you do? Here's one example of how neutral language might work in this situation.

Subject: Doughnut Debacle
From: Dan Davies
Date: October 15
To: Jim Smith

Dear Mr. Smith:

Our apologies for the mistake involving your recent daiquiri-flavored doughnut order. We believe this error occurred due to a computer glitch involving a sugar-glazed doughnut with sprinkles and a spilled cup of coffee. We will do what we can to make this right. Please consider our offer to overnight the correct doughnuts to you, at our cost, as a formal apology for the mistake.

Yours truly,
Dan Davies
Head Doughnut Maker

7

Make Your E-Mails Action-Packed

If you want your e-mails to be jam-packed with action, you have no better friend than the verb. Loading up your messages with language that promotes accomplishments to be achieved, tasks to be undertaken, and problems to be solved will make things happen.

Although certainly not a complete list, the following is a cheat sheet of power verbs you can use to bring movement to your messages.

Verbs that relate to the creative process			
Built Constructed Directed Generated Originated Produced	Composed Created Established Initiated Performed Revised	Conceived Designed Formulated Invented Piloted	Conceptualized Developed Founded Launched Planned

Verbs that relate to leadership			
Achieved Effected Headed Led Presided	Clarified Enhanced Improved Marketed Recommended	Decided Exceeded Inspired Motivated Succeeded	Delegated Excelled Instigated Participated
Verbs that relate to research			
Analyzed Compared Experimented Interviewed Studied	Clarified Contrasted Explored Investigated Summarized	Coded Evaluated Inquired Reported Surveyed	Collected Examined Interpreted Reviewed
Verbs that relate to teaching, coaching, and mentoring			
Advised Clarified Counseled Directed Facilitated Instructed Planned Trained	Advocated Coached Demonstrated Educated Guided Inspired Represented Tutored	Assessed Collaborated Developed Encouraged Illustrated Led Served	Assisted Conducted Diagnosed Explained Informed Mentored Supported
Verbs that relate to communication			
Advertised Composed Drafted Interpreted Notified Proofread Wrote	Arbitrated Contacted Edited Mediated Presented Publicized	Authored Corresponded Facilitated Moderated Persuaded Published	Clarified Demonstrated Informed Negotiated Promoted Translated

Verbs that relate to management and organization			
Administered	Arranged	Assembled	Completed
Conducted	Controlled	Correlated	Determined
Directed	Eliminated	Engineered	Evaluated
Executed	Expanded	Implemented	Increased
Maintained	Managed	Planned	Prepared
Procured	Provided	Scheduled	Solved
Supervised			
Verbs that relate to technical issues			
Analyzed	Budgeted	Built	Calculated
Computed	Correlated	Developed	Financed
Handled	Maintained	Manipulated	Operated
Programmed	Repaired		

8

Make Effective Requests

Most of the e-mails you send ask another person to take some kind of action, such as sending invoice information, giving feedback on a proposed project, or confirming attendance at an upcoming meeting. How well your e-mail elicits the response you desire has everything to do with how effectively you've crafted your request. A well-written request consists of three major ingredients.

Detailed action. Imagine receiving an e-mail from your boss asking for a list of all the new customer accounts in the past six months. You diligently go about gathering the information: sorting the data into size of client, location of offices, frequency and type of sales, contact information, and so on. Once you have printed and bound the document, you present it to your boss, who looks at you as if you are crazy, and says, "I just needed an overhead containing client names for the quarterly meeting tomorrow." Aaaaggghhh!

If your boss had been more specific, and asked for a one-page overview of new clients closed in the past six months, the boss would have gotten what he or she wanted, and you would have been saved time and irritation.

Hot Hint

If you receive an e-mail request in which the action is open to interpretation, save yourself time and trouble by asking the requestor for more definite details.

Specific time frame. Because they signify different things to different people, terms such as *soon*, *immediately*, *when you get a chance*, and *as soon as possible* should be used sparingly. For example, when you write *immediately* in an e-mail, you might mean "drop everything and do this now." The receiver might translate the same word to mean "as soon as I have finished what I am working on." If you have a tight deadline, the difference between these two interpretations could be the difference between success and failure.

To avoid any confusion, always state time frames in clear, unambiguous terms such as "at 3 p.m. tomorrow," "today by noon," "on Wednesday, January 23, at 10 a.m.," and so on.

Mutual understanding. Many times when you make a request, the other person knows exactly what you are talking about because you are both aware of the background and circumstances involved. For example, if you sent an e-mail to a coworker who has been assisting you in creating a new Website, a request such as "Please call the Web designer today and make sure she has everything she needs" would be acceptable because the "needs" are known by both of you. There is no need for clarification because you mutually understand what is involved. However, if you sent the same request to a coworker who had no knowledge of the project, you would need to go into greater detail in the e-mail, so that the request could be fulfilled satisfactorily.

Exercise

Read the following four examples of requests. Rate each of them based upon how effective they would be in getting the desired result.

1. *I hope you received the e-mail I sent you yesterday with the preliminary design plans for the new reception area. I'd appreciate it if you could take a look at them when you get a moment.*

☐ Poor ☐ Okay ☐ Good ☐ Great

Why?

____

____

2. *Next week I will be out on vacation so it's important that I receive all unprocessed orders by end of day tomorrow (Thursday, August 21). Any orders that I do not receive tomorrow will have to wait until I get back, which will be Monday, September 1st. If you have any questions, please feel free to contact me before noon on Friday, August 22.*

☐ Poor ☐ Okay ☐ Good ☐ Great

9

Use the E.M.A.I.L. Acronym

If you want a quick way to check up on your priority-one e-mails, prior to posting them for the entire world to see, try the E.M.A.I.L.

acronym. Going through these few steps before you hit the *send* button will save you time and tension in the long run.

E = Effective Writing

Is your message one run-together text, or is it formatted in paragraphs, making it easier to read?

Is your e-mail written clearly and concisely, with the most important facts upfront in the first paragraph?

Have you checked for spelling, grammar, and typos?

M = Message Tone

Have you avoided using all caps, which could be construed as "flaming" or shouting?

Are you conveying a professional and friendly tone?

Are there any parts of your message that could be misinterpreted or misconstrued?

Have you made a clear request? If not, is this e-mail just an FYI?

A = Appropriateness

Is e-mail the right medium for this message?

Does the message contain anything that might be better communicated in person?

Is this message urgent, and better dealt with over the phone?

Does this message contain credit card details, Social Security numbers, salary information, rumors, hearsay, or anything that might be of an inflammatory nature?

I = Impact on Others

Is the subject line of this message clear and specific?

Did I include a greeting and sign-off?

Have I limited the CC to those people who need to receive this e-mail?

L = Legal

Do you know and understand your company's electronic communications policies, and does this e-mail meet those?

Does this e-mail contain anything that could be considered trade secrets, intellectual property, or security-sensitive material?

Does this e-mail contain anything inappropriate for which you could be dismissed?

Is their anything in this e-mail that could be used as evidence in a court of law?

10

Say No With Style

No one likes to hear that they can't have what they want when they want it, which is why saying that little two-letter word—*no*—can be such a difficult and uncomfortable task. Unfortunately, in today's world, federal regulations, legal issues, company policies, and just plain old no-can-do, often make it impossible for you to say yes to all the customer, vendor, and coworker requests you receive.

When it comes to e-mail, nothing turns a necessary *no* into a needless message with bad manners faster than an online decline poorly executed. Often called a *hard no*, this is the type of *nada* that provides no possibility for problem resolution and offers no empathy or options, or expression of desire to help.

Consider the following example taken from two actual e-mails.

A potential client sees an ad for travel services on the Internet and sends an e-mail to the company selling the services. The potential client's e-mail reads:

Dear Sirs,

I am interested in your travel services, which I saw advertised on the Web. Can you please tell me if you offer accreditation as a travel agent as well?

The response from the company:

Dear Miss,

I have no way of knowing that. The offer is as advertised. Nothing more, nothing less.

A classic *hard no* if ever there was one—and impolite to boot! Like it or not, from time to time you will have to send an e-mail that says no. When this happens, use a *service no* to create a more successful outcome and maintain customer and coworker relationships. A *service no* does not attempt to make a no sound like a yes, but rather offers workable options, alternatives, and empathy.

Exercise

Think about a situation in which you need to e-mail someone and decline his or her request or offer. In the space provided, write a few sentences conveying your no. Read through your decline and write down how you think the tone of that e-mail will come across to the person reading it?

Hard No:

____

____

____

How do I think the reader will respond to this?

____

____

____

Now, rewrite your decline using a few phrases from the Service No list following. How do you think this rewritten version will come across to the reader?

Service No:

____

____

____

How do I think the reader will respond to this?

____

____

____

Hard No	Service No
I/You can't do that	What I can do is
I cannot help you	It might be possible to
That's not my job	I can recommend
That's not our policy	Another option is
There's no way	I have an alternative idea
You're on your own	What you can do is

11

Engage the Expressive Style

With a deep desire to engage others, build alliances, and create excitement, goal-oriented individuals persuade others with their passion. Their e-mail style can best be described as Expressive. They take an enthusiastic approach to their e-mail messages by:

- Expressing their opinions strongly.
- Using motivational language.
- Projecting an enthusiastic tone.
- Focusing on the up side.
- Painting a broad picture.

Consider this typical Expressive-style e-mail.

Subject: Holiday Client Gifts
From: Julie Gotaloveit
Date: November 20
To: Sales Team

Hi gang!

The holidays are almost here, and many of you have talked to me about how excited you are to give your best clients gifts this year.

I share your enthusiasm for both our clients and gift-giving. However, we need to put our heads together, brainstorm, and figure out how to overcome the obstacle of this year's budget cuts.

I have no doubt that, working together, we will come up with a solution to this problem, so that our much-deserving clients can get a holiday gift this year.

The best way to respond to this style is with:

- Energy and enthusiasm.
- Excitement about the ideas.
- A focus on the big picture.
- Support from people the writer respects.

Consider this response to an Expressive e-mail style.

From: Tina Tiny
Subject: Holiday Client Gifts
Date: November 21
To: Julie Gotaloveit

Dear Julie:

You bet!

First off, let me say I could not agree more; together we can figure this out.

I already spoke with Larry, with whom you used to work in accounting, and he has tons of ideas to run by you.

Some of them have to do with a fundraiser, a few focus on the mad money account...you get the picture.

How about if we set up a brainstorming meeting for next week to iron out these ideas?

Let me know if this will work for you, and again, I know we will find a solution.

12

Step Into the Straight-Shooter Style

Certain people at work always have their eyes on the prize and know exactly what they want and how they want to get there. These results-oriented individuals like to win and don't like to waste time mincing words. Their e-mail style can be described as a Straight Shooter. Often feeling overwhelmed by work, the writer with this style:

- Gets to the point quickly.
- Makes direct requests.
- Uses forceful language.
- May pressure you to act quickly.
- Can be abrupt in tone.
- Does not invite feedback or discussion.

Consider this typical Straight Shooter–style e-mail.

Subject: Holiday Client Gifts
From: Jim Arrow
Date: November 20
To: Sales Team

Dear Sales Team:

I understand that some of you are planning on giving company holiday gifts to our largest clients this season. I am not in favor of this for the following reasons:

1. Given our budget cuts, cost containment is necessary.
2. It is too difficult to decide where to cut the list.

If you feel you must do this, write me with your reason, the client, and what you want to give them, ASAP.

The best way to respond to this style is to:

- Give straight answers back, straight away.
- Write action-oriented e-mails that provide only relevant information.
- Be as concise as possible.

If a topic is more complex than you can quickly cover in an e-mail, you might want to schedule an in-person meeting.

Consider the response to a Straight Shooter–type e-mail following.

From: Tina Tiny
Subject: Holiday Client Gifts
Date: November 21
To: Jim Arrow

Dear Jim:

I would like an exception to the holiday gift policy.

My client, Jones Shirtsleeves, increased their busines with us by 500% this year. This represents a dollar amount of $50,000 to our company. I want to spend $50 on a gift.

I look forward to your response.

13

Ease Into the Nice and Easy Style

There are those people with whom we work who are feeling-oriented folks who will take the time to chat about casual topics both on- and offline. Building rapport and team problem-solving are high on their list of workplace priorities. As writers, their style can best be described as Nice and Easy. They take a personal and friendly approach to e-mail by:

- Expressing their feelings.
- Using inspirational quotes.
- Using conversational language.
- Inviting feedback and discussion.
- Writing in description and detail.

Consider this typical Nice and Easy–style e-mail.

Subject: Holiday Client Gifts
From: Candy Candycane
Date: November 20th
To: Sales Team

Dear Sales Team:

Well, the holidays are just around the corner! I know many of you have been thinking about the holiday gifts you might give to your clients this year. Sadly, I have a few concerns I want to share with you regarding this.

First, let me say that our clients are the greatest group of people in the world. But as you know with the budget cuts this year, I fear we just won't have the resources to send out gifts. I worry about where to draw the line and hurting certain clients' feelings.

I want to hear from each and every one of you regarding your feelings on this matter. I am quite certain that together, as a team, we will solve this problem.

Just remember, within every problem lies an opportunity.

The best way to respond to this style is to:

- Use a friendly and upbeat tone.
- Start with a personal greeting upfront.
- Use feeling language.
- Make suggestions rather than demands.

Consider this response to a Nice and Easy–type e-mail.

From: Tina Tiny
Subject: Holiday Client Gifts
Date: November 21
To: Candy Candycane

Dear Candy:

Thanks for your great e-mail about the upcoming hoiday season.

I share your feelings and want to make things the best they can be for our wonderful clients.

My suggestion is that we have a morning meeting next week to come up with a list of the clients to whom we feel it would be most important to give gifts this season. If you agree, I'll bring the coffee and cookies!

Let me know what you think, and thanks again.

14

Be Part of the Problem-Solving Style

There is a whole group of nice, professional people in the workplace whose job it is to focus on logic, detail, fact, and figures. These task-oriented individuals concentrate on concrete realities, not abstract feelings. Their e-mail style can best be described as Problem-Solving. They take a "just the facts" approach to e-mail by:

- Choosing their words carefully.
- Using neutral language.
- Projecting a serious tone.
- Laying out their logic and thinking.
- Discussing details.

Consider this typical Problem-Solving-style e-mail.

Subject: Holiday Client Gifts
From: Larry Logic
Date: November 20
To: Sales Team

To all Sales Team members:

In exactly 24 days, Chrismas will arrive. I have spoken with 14 out of the 15 team members, and with the exception of John in accounting, you have all stated your intention to give holiday gifts to your top 10% of clients.

I am writing to inform you that due to our 30% reduction in budget this year, holiday gifts will not be possible.

Please suspend any plans you currently have to provide gifts to your client base. If you have an exeption, send me a detailed e-mail with the relevant information by November 25.

I will make a determination and get back to you with a response by November 30.

The best way to respond to this style is to:

- Back up your position with facts, not feelings.
- Get straight to the point.
- Use neutral language.
- Explain logically why your idea has validity.

Consider the response to the following Problem-Solving-type e-mail.

From: Tina Tiny
Subject: Holiday Client Gifts
Date: November 21
To: Larry Logic

Larry:

I received your e-mail today regarding the suspension of holiday gifts for clients.

Per you instructions I am submitting my request for an exception within the dates specified. The facts are as follows:

1. My client, Jones Johnson, has increased his business with us five-fold this year, up from $50,000 to $250,000.

2. Our profit margins on this account have stayed the same, at 45.6%.
3. The gift I am considering will cost $50.00. This is 0.2% of overall sales form this client.

If you look at the numbers, this a low-cost way to say we appreciate his business.

If you have any questions, please let me know. If not, I will expect your response by the 30th.

— —

15

Start With a Salutation

Most people give a greeting at the drop of a hat. For instance, they say *hello* when answering the phone; they offer a *nice to meet you* when being introduced to someone new, and start a letter with *Dear*. Why, then, do so many people launch into their e-mail messages without even an acknowledgment of the other person's name? Remember, your e-mail's salutation in a small way helps to set the tone for the message to come.

Obviously, e-mails sent to family and friends can be more casual than those sent to customers, coworkers, and vendors. Salutations to close pals might include such classics as *Yo!*, *Howdy*, and *What's up?*

Business associates, however, usually require a more formal greeting. Consciously crafting a salutation is a mental reminder that you are speaking to another person rather than just typing words on a screen—something that's easy to forget in today's fast-paced world.

The most usual salutation is *Dear*, followed by the recipient's first or last name, depending on your relationship. Some e-mail correspondents forgo the *Dear* altogether and just write the recipient's name followed by a colon. This is a less formal approach, and should be reserved for people with whom you have a well-established relationship.

When responding to e-mails you receive from people you don't know well, look for the following clues to tell you how you should refer to them when writing back.

- If the person signs off with his or her full name (Carol Carmichael), be on the safe side and reply *Dear Ms. Carmichael.*
- If a woman does not denote her marital status (Carol Carmichael), then go with *Ms.*
- If the person signs off with his or her first name (Carol), you can feel free to respond in kind with *Dear Carol.*
- If the person signs off with a title (Dr. Carol Carmichael), always use the title in your response, as in *Dear Dr. Carmichael.*

Hot Hint

If *Dear* just isn't your thing, and you know the person, or have a less formal relationship, you can always go with *Hello Harold*, *Hi Harold*, or just plain old *Harold*.

Once you've sorted out the greeting, the few words after the salutation provide the equivalent of the *Nice to meet you* exchange that is the customary opener to any usual face-to-face and telephone conversation. Useful e-mail opening lines include:

- Thank you for your note, e-mail, message, and so on.
- I hope this e-mail is finding you well.
- I trust you had a pleasant weekend, holiday, vacation, or the like.

- Good day/morning/afternoon/evening.
- I was referred to you by [fill in the blank].
- Please allow me to introduce myself.

Group Greetings

When sending a message to an entire group, rather than an individual, offer a group greeting such as:

- Hi All
- Greetings
- Hello Everyone
- Dear Team Members
- Dear Friends/Colleagues/Associates
- Dear Clients

16

Craft a Compelling Subject Line

As straightforward as an e-mail subject line seems, it can serve a variety of purposes. A well-written subject line can inform readers, entice them to take action, inspire them to buy, or engage their curiosity.

There is no doubt that how you brand your e-mail to customers, clients, coworkers, and vendors has an impact on whether they decide to open or delete your e-mail. Here are just a few things to consider when crafting your subject line.

Make it compelling, not cute. Read through your e-mail and identify the most valuable content. What topic would capture the receivers' interest and make them want to read on? Make that your subject line.

Compelling: *I want your valuable input at Tuesday's sales meeting.*

Cute: *Don't miss out on having your say-so.*

Avoid sounding like spam. Keep your readers from being skeptical by steering clear of a subject line that sounds as though it's promoting a product or service they didn't ask for, and probably don't want. For example, consider these spam-sounding subject lines:

Proven Program—Enlarge Your Brain

Well-Made Replica Watches

Work From Home—Earn Thousands

Say Goodbye to Debt Forever

Keep them short and to the point. As a general rule of thumb, the shorter your e-mail subject line, the better. Because the average subject line displays about 35 to 50 characters, make those first few words really count, and grab the reader right upfront. For example, change the average-sounding subject line *5 great Bay Area Picnic Spots* into the more compelling *Hot Picnic Spots—Bay Area's 5 Best.*

Make it immediate. If your e-mail is time sensitive and you want to encourage the reader to open it immediately, have the subject line reflect this. For example:

Celebrity Signed Picnic Baskets—Today Only.

Emphasize benefit over offer. What does your subject line say about the specific benefit the reader will receive by opening your e-mail? Instead of just listing your offer or a feature, make the value proposition clear. For example:

Offer only: *New Study On Exercise*

Benefit: *Live Five Years Longer With Exercise*

Use the newspaper rule. If you want a quick lesson in how to write attention-grabbing, to the point, information-packed subject lines, just pick up any major newspaper. Headlines are the newspaper equivalent of e-mail subject lines. Ask yourself: *If this e-mail were a story in a newspaper and needed a headline, what would it be?*

Use 10 Tips. Some research suggests that subject lines containing a specific number of tips are opened more frequently. For example:

10 Tips For A Better Golf Swing

Five Ways To Lose Weight

Match the e-mail content. Have you ever received an e-mail on which the subject line was from a previous topic and has nothing to do with the current message? As the content of your e-mails change, change the subject lines accordingly.

Avoid saying too little. Consider the following subject headings:

Following Up

About Allison

Invoices

Although you might have a vague idea of what these cryptic subject lines refer to, they really provide no information and no reason to open them for the recipient—at least not with any urgency. Instead, by adding just a bit more specific information you encourage the reader to open. For example:

Following Up becomes *New Sales Proposal—Did You Read Yet?*

About Allison becomes *Allison Anderson Just Promoted to V.P.*

Invoices becomes *Invoice From Washington Trip Due by Thursday*

Subject Line No-No's

There are a few words and phrases that are so often used by spammers, recipients will target your e-mail as spam if you use them, even if it's not. Some subject line killers include the words *limited time*, *free*, *opportunity*, *only*, and *you*.

Exercise

Open your e-mail inbox and read through the first 10 subject lines you see. How good a job did they do in the following areas?

- Left no confusion as to what exactly the e-mail was about.
- Were pithy and to the point.
- Made you want to open them and read further.
- Were on track and on target with the content of the e-mail.

Now, open your sent box and read through the first 10 subject lines of the e-mails you see. How good a job did you do in each of those areas? How could you have improved your subject lines? Use the space following to rewrite any if necessary.

17

Sign Off With Substance

Just as the salutation helps set the tone for the beginning of the e-mail, the sign-off brings your message to a close with the proper mood. Think of your goodbye as the period at the end of a sentence.

Whereas sign-offs to friends and family are often casual (*see ya, later, gotta go*), sign-offs with business associates, or people you don't know well, are best left on a more formal note. For example:

- Regards
- Sincerely
- Thank you
- Thanks
- See you soon
- Look forward to seeing you soon
- Hope to hear from you soon
- Best
- Best wishes

If you're one of those people who likes to end your e-mails with your name or just the initial of your first name, that's fine, but save it for folks with whom you have a close rapport.

Equally important to your close is the inclusion of an automatic electronic signature file that ends each and every message with critical information about where you can be reached. A basic signature line will usually include the following information:

- Your name
- Your title and/or position
- Your company name
- Your mailing address
- Your fax number
- Your phone number
- Your e-mail address
- The URL for your Website

Here's an example.

Subject: Potato Salad for Company Picnic
From: Susan Shinehold
Date: July 13
To: Paddy Peeler

Dear Paddy;

Hi. Just checking in to see if you are available to make your world-class potato salad for about 100 people at this year's company picnic. Of course all potatoes and mayonnaise will be provided. Let me know if you can accommodate this request.

Regards,
Susan

Susan Shinehold, President
The Potato Council
1800 Spud Lane #200
Boise, Idaho 83701
Phone (208) 333-9898
Fax (208) 333-9899
www.spudsareus.com

"A Potato a Day Keeps the Blues Away"

Hot Hint

If you decide to include a quote as a part of your signature line, keep it short, relevant, and neutral. FYI: Most programs allow you to create several different signature files so that you can pick and choose the most appropriate one for each e-mail communication.

They Know Who I Am

An e-mail that lacks a signature line is like a voice-mail missing a phone number.

Don't assume that everyone has your information at their fingertips. Need some more motivation to create one? Consider these:

- It's free advertisement.
- It saves the other person the time of having to look up your information.
- It looks more professional.
- It's the courteous thing to do.
- It lets people click through to your Website.

18

Go Easy on the CC

Too often, too many e-mails find their way onto the desktops of unsuspecting colleagues who don't really need to be in the loop on this or that conversation.

The ease of CCing (carbon copying/courtesy copying) a co-worker or employee makes it temping to throw caution to the wind and communicate at large. If you want to be thought of as a model of e-mail restraint, resist this temptation, and use the CC function with caution. A few things to keep in mind include:

A CC message works best on a need-to-know basis. If a second (third, or fourth) person needs to be updated, or informed of the information being sent to your main recipient, then the CC function works well. For example: You are e-mailing the company-picnic team leader with suggestions for fun activities for the up-coming outing. You also CC his boss, who told you yesterday he would be happy to participate in the Dunk the Clown Booth.

Understand the difference between "To" and "CC." In general, the person you send the e-mail "To" is the one you expect to take any action you have requested. Unless you specifically ask for it, don't expect the "CC" recipient to even respond to the message.

Alphabetize the list of CC recipients. Organizations being political animals, and people being easily offended, if you are CCing more than just one person, do it alphabetically to avoid any hint of hierarchy.

Don't CC anyone who may not be sure why they are being included. Being CC'd on an e-mail can be confusing to the recipient if he or she doesn't know why you have copied him or her, or what you expect him or her to do with the information. If you think there might be confusion, mention your reason for the CC in the e-mail.

For example:

Subject: Upcoming Company Picnic
From: Bruce Barneby
Date: May 15
To: Barney Bails
CC: Bob Barn, Billy Bubblehead, Jim Carpenski

Dear Barney;

Let me say again how happy I am that you have been assigned to be the team leader for this year's company picnic project. As you requested, I have listed below several suggestions for activities. They include:

- Dunk the Clown (your boss Bob has agreed to participate)
- Cotton Candy–Making booth
- Chicken Races
- Hot-Dog-Eating Contest (Jim in accounting was a national champion—who knew?!)
- Snow Cone Pitching Tent

FYI, as it turns out, Billy Bubblehead used to work for the circus and has offered his services.

Let me know if I can be of any further assistance, and please feel free to contact Bob, Billy, or Jim directly, if they can help.

Yours,
Bruce

To CC Back or Not?

When you receive a message that has also been CC'd to one or more people, should you hit *Reply All*, or send a solo response back? This depends on the situation, but a good rule of thumb is to only CC back those people you want to see your reply for a specific reason. Ask yourself, "Would this person want or need to see my response?"

19

BCC With Caution

On occasion you may choose to use the BCC (blind carbon copy) function. This allows you to send the same message you sent to the main recipient, without that person knowing you sent it to anyone else. A few situations for which the BCC may be your best option include:

When you want to keep the CC list confidential. If you don't want the primary recipient to know to whom else you have sent your message, a BCC will hide that information. Be warned, however, that if the primary recipient finds out, it can appear as if you were trying to go behind his or her back.

One corporate client in our Essential E-mail seminar reported that she had been BCC'd by her boss on a department problem, without realizing that it was a BCC. She responded by hitting the "Reply All" button, unintentionally setting off a hailstorm of conflict between the sender and the original recipient, who had no idea about the BCC.

When a regular CC would cause confusion. If you want a coworker to be in on the particulars of a customer, vendor, or colleague communication, but the intended party would be confused as to why someone else is being CC'd—use the BCC option.

When you want to protect privacy. When you use the CC field, everyone on the list can see everyone else's e-mail address. Doing this runs the risk of irritating and even offending those who don't want their e-mail addresses made public. This is especially true when you are including the e-mail addresses of clients. When in doubt, use the BCC option to protect confidentiality.

When you have a large list. If you have a large list and don't want to overwhelm (or annoy) your readers with having to view it, use the BCC option.

When you want to prevent data mining. If you are at all concerned that the people to whom you are sending the message, or CCing the message, might use the list to inappropriately contact, market, or try to sell the recipients, go the BCC route.

When revealing the other person might cause stress. On those occasions when you want to keep someone in the loop, but you don't want the person for whom the e-mail is intended to be intimidated by that fact, you might use the BCC function. For example: The vice president of your division wants to keep close tabs on a special project you have one of your staff working on, but you don't want the staff member to feel as though the big boss is breathing down his or her neck.

If at any time you find yourself feeling guilty, embarrassed, or nervous about BCCing someone, then don't. This includes BCCing as a way to punish, harass, or tarnish another's reputation.

When you need other people to know about the situation. Even if the main reader would be upset to know that other people were CC'd in on the conversation, if you need to keep others informed, you may want to send a summary of the situation to the other people involved, rather than CC the actual e-mail. For all involved, it would be best if you let the recipient know you have done this.

20

Consider Attachment Options

These days most businesses couldn't function without the ability to send files attached to e-mail messages. The author who sends his completed chapters to the publisher, the musician who sends her sound files to a producer, or the photographer who sends his pictures to a magazine—all have the option to transmit their data instantly via e-mail.

As efficient as sending attachments can be, there are some important things to consider before distributing them.

Size

Even the post office and your friendly parcel carrier have size limits on what they can deliver. Just as you wouldn't expect the mailman to be able to drop off a dining room table on your doorstep, you can't expect e-mail to deal with overly large attachments (those larger than 2 megabytes). One reason is that many recipients don't have enough space in their mailboxes to receive these oversized files. Most word-processing documents don't pose a problem, but sending 200 photos of Bertie in accounting's retirement party to your colleague could be. Err on the safe side and assume that any attachment larger than 1 or 2 megabytes might be a problem.

If you *must* send *every* picture of Bertie's big bash, here are two options.

Compress the images. If you have a Windows Operating System, a program such as "Winzip" takes all the attached files and compresses them into a tight little bundle. When they arrive at the other end, they can be quickly decompressed or "unstuffed" and viewed. If you're using an Apple machine, "Stuffit" is the most popular compression software.

Send several smaller e-mails. Break the attachment into several bite-sized pieces, and send each one attached to a separate e-mail. This is only a practical alternative if the file is easy to segment. For example, sending 200 separate e-mails, each with one Bertie picture, would be laborious and time-consuming.

Use a server. One method that bypasses attachments altogether is to upload your files to a server that is then accessed via the Web by your recipient, who can then download them. Popular services include YouSendIt and FilesAnywhere. For photographic storage try Photobucket and Shutterfly.

Security

Before sending any attachment, ask yourself, "Is there anything in this document that is private and not for everyone's eyes?" If the answer is yes, then find an alternate method of delivery. There are too many cases of identity theft and industrial espionage that are a direct result of someone carelessly transmitting sensitive information.

21

Open Attachments With Care

It may be hard to believe, but there are people out there who spend their lives looking for ways to mess with your computer. Viruses, worms, and Trojan horses are all computer bugs that can make mincemeat of your electronic files, and they are usually hidden away in a harmless-looking attachment. A few best practices to follow regarding attachments you receive include the following.

Before opening an attachment, always verify that it's one you are expecting or from a person you know.

To be safe, invest in antivirus software—preferably one that has an update feature that ensures you have protection for the very latest evildoers. Norton Antivirus, McAfee, and Intego VirusBarrier are some of the products you might want to check out.

To make the opening of attachments easier, use a PDF format. The widespread use of PDF (Portable Document Format) files has brought about more format compatibility. For example, without PDF, a file created in Adobe Illustrator can only be opened as an attachment by a computer that has that programmed installed. If, however, the original file is converted to a PDF format, it can be opened by any computer that has a PDF reader, with all the graphics and formatting preserved.

Hot Hint

If you receive an attachment that is not a PDF, JPEG, or GIF (commonly supported formats for text and graphics), and you cannot open it, then use the letters at the end of the file name to determine the native program that created it. For example, a Microsoft Word document ends with *.doc*, an Excel document ends with *.xls*, and *.ai* are the call letters for Adobe Illustrator. To find out what letters belong to what programs, go to *www.ace.net.nz/tech/TechFileFormat.html* for a complete listing.

I Love You, I Love You Not!

One high-profile virus arrived in an e-mail with the subject line *I love you*. Attached was a document called Love Letter. Once opened, the virus would send a copy of itself to everyone on the user's address list, as if sent by the user. It also made a series of nasty changes to the systems it infected. The virus appeared on May 4, 2000, in the Philippines, spread across the world in less than 24 hours, and affected 10 percent of all online computers. The Pentagon, CIA, British Parliament, and most corporations had to shut down their e-mail in order to eliminate the virus. Total damage for the day was estimated to be $5.5 billion.

22

Shorten Your Sentences

Stretched out sentences that go on forever are an e-mail no-no. Case in point, the long, laborious sentence following.

Sentences that make point after point can really strain the reader's patience and make you look like you don't know how to say anything with the brevity and conciseness required in today's short-attention-span world, which is a big problem if you want to be seen as an effective professional.

If you find yourself face-to-face with such a run-on sentence, use the following tips to shorten it.

Eliminate conjunctions. A conjunction is a word that joins together words and phrases. Words such as *for, and, but, or, yet,* and *so* are common conjunctions. One way to shorten your sentences is to remove them, and turn one long sentence into two shorter ones. For example:

- Long sentence with conjunction: *I thought it might be fun to go out to lunch on Wednesday and to discuss where to hold our next company off-site, or just get caught up.*
- Shorter sentence with the conjunction *and* removed: *I thought it might be fun to go out to lunch on Wednesday. We can discuss where to hold our next company off-site, or just get caught up.*

Hot Hint

The most readable sentences contain 10 to 17 words.

Remove transitions. A transition is a word or phrase that holds your various ideas together. Common transitions include: *To point out, with this in mind, although, for instance.* Too many transitions can create run-on sentences and confusion. For example:

- Long sentence with transitions: *We all need to study the new safety rules instituted at work this week; with this in mind, we will be having a meeting on Friday.*
- Shorter sentence with the transition *with this in mind* removed: *We all need to study the new safety rules instituted at work this week. We will be having a meeting on Friday.*

Say it simpler. The use of too many words can make a sentence lose focus and cause a reader to lose interest. One way to prune your prose is to be more direct and to the point.

Exercise

Take the following long sentence and break it up into three separate, shorter ones.

"Whenever our supervisors bring in pizza or take us out for lunch it's often a sign of us either having to put in a lot of unexpected overtime or that we are going to be given bad news and they want to soften the blow as much as possible so that we don't all start complaining and talking to each other instead of working."

____

____

____

How did you do? Check out the following suggestions.

Sentence #1: Whenever our supervisors bring in pizza or take us out for lunch it's often a bad sign.

Sentence #2: It can mean a lot of unexpected overtime or some other bad news.

Sentence #3: Our bosses try to soften the blow as much as possible so that we don't all start complaining and talking to each other instead of working.

23

Vary Your Sentence Length

Sentences that are all one length can be monotonous. They have no variety, and are often boring. They tend to make the reader fall asleep. You want to avoid writing sentences like this. If you do, you run the risk of being dull.

Can you see this from the examples we just used?

The liveliest e-mails include a variety of sentence lengths. Some are short; some are longer. By varying the length of your e-mail sentences, you create a more interesting tempo and add impact to your message. Here are a few things to keep in mind when crafting your sentences.

Short sentences are more expressive and energetic in nature than long sentences, and work well for presenting concise thoughts or ideas. For example:

- *The network is down.*
- *We closed the deal.*
- *Way to go!*
- *He said what?*

Long sentences are better suited to explore possibilities, elaborate on ideas, or present involved concepts. For example:

- *We find that most companies understand the importance of customer satisfaction surveys, yet only a few know how to really leverage the information to increase both sales and loyalty.*

- *Although we all know the problems that can arise when customers call in and cannot reach the person that can best solve their problems, we haven't ever been willing to allocate resources to solving this service failure.*

Exercise

The following paragraph contains sentences of approximately the same length. Notice how the words deliver the message, but the tempo is flat:

"As you all know, yesterday the network went down for two hours. The cause of the problem was a server that went off-line. We are trying to discover why the failsafe back-ups did not switch in. I will let you know more information as I get it. Thank you all for doing whatever was needed to handle the situation."

Please rewrite the paragraph, using varying sentence lengths.

____

____

____

____

____

____

How does your rewrite compare with the following sample?

"As you all know, yesterday the network was off-line for two hours because a server went down. The backup didn't switch in. We are trying to discover why the failure occurred, and I will let you know as soon as I know. You all did a remarkable job. Thank you all for doing whatever it took."

24

Choose Your Sentence Style With Care

Depending on their tone, sentences can enlighten, entertain, educate, and, on occasion, even annoy. The right combination of sentence styles can be the difference between an e-mail that sings and one that falls flat. For shorter e-mails, one or two sentence types will usually fit the bill, but for longer, more complicated e-mails, a mixture works magic. The following are five basic sentence styles and some suggestions on how to use them to their best advantage.

Declarative sentences. These are sentences that simply state a fact or argument without asking the reader to take any action or choose sides either way. More often than not, they end with the plain old period. For example:

- *I needed to work this weekend to get the report done.*
- *I will be in my cubicle by 1 p.m. Monday.*
- *I like peaches.*

Exclamatory sentences. A more forceful version of a declarative statement, these express strong opinions and surprise at facts. They feel as if they should (and often do) end with an exclamation point. For example:

- *I had to work all weekend—morning, noon, and night—to get that report done!*
- *I've earned the right to take Monday morning off!*
- *Peaches are the best fruit in the whole wide world!*

Imperative sentences. Usually beginning with a verb, these sentences give a direct command to someone or ask for action. For example:

- *Sit down for this.*
- *Read this report for tomorrow.*
- *Take messages for me until I return.*
- *Consider your options.*

Interrogative sentences. These sentences ask questions and usually begin with *can*, *who*, *why*, *will*, *when*, or *how*, and they always end with a question mark. For example:

- *Will you please get me a double-decaf-mocha-latte-no-foam from the cafeteria?*
- *How many times have I gone over this with Bill?*
- *Does X mark the spot?*

Rhetorical sentences. These are statements posed as questions, but not really meant for the reader to answer. When used sparingly, these types of sentences can add some flavor to an e-mail. For example:

- *Why do we always seem to find ourselves in this situation?*
- *Is he serious?*
- *What is up with that?*

Stream-of-consciousness sentences. A by-product of the online age, these sentences don't really follow the rules of good grammar and are characterized by their free and loose style. For example:

- *Wow, what a day...I had to deal with the dog...but that's another story. Anyway, I got through it and now I'm working on my upcoming vacation....France, I can't wait...by the way, how's your vacation plans coming?*

Clearly, this type of sentence structure should only be used for casual, informal e-mails with people you know very well.

Exercise

Using the following information, write an e-mail that incorporates at least three of the sentence styles we outlined.

1. This e-mail is from you to a coworker about your upcoming vacation.
2. You need to have your top accounts covered while you are away.
3. Your coworker is overwhelmed and already has too much to do.
4. You will be gone on vacation for one week only.

25

Put the Apostrophe in Its Place

Is this Uncle Jack's pen? All the purple pens' caps are loose. Where did Jim, Jack, and Jason's pen go? How did Jim's, Jack's, and Jason's pens perform?

There are so many apostrophes, but just a few rules. In general, the apostrophe is used in these six ways:

#1: When you want a singular noun to express ownership, use the apostrophe to hold the *s* in place. For example:

- Singular noun: Bob
- What he owns: Happiness
- How to use the apostrophe: Jane basked in *Bob's* happiness
- Test: Does the word *of* express what you want to say? As in "the happiness of Bob"?

#2: When you want to express plural ownership, because the plural of most English nouns ends with an *s*, place the apostrophe at the end. For example:

- The *birds'* happiness is apparent in their sweet tweet.
- Many *pens'* black ink.
- Three *days'* deliberation.

#3: To show possession shared by more than one noun, add the apostrophe and the *s* to the last noun in the series. For example: Jim, Jack, and Jason's pen.

#4: However, if the possession is individual, add the apostrophe and *s* to each player in the game. For example: Jane's, Bob's, and the bird's sounds all seem sweet.

#5: Pronominal possessives such as *hers*, *its*, *theirs*, *yours*, and *ours* do not have an apostrophe to show possession. For example: The cat cleans *its* ears.

#6: To form the plural of a letter, a number or a sign, omit the apostrophe and just add an *s*. For example:

- Mind your *Ps* and *Qs*
- Jane remembers the *1960s* with fondness
- Call me in the morning with your sales *#s*.

Note: Depending on whether you follow the *Chicago Manual of Style*, as this book does, or the *AP Stylebook*, there are some differences in rules. For example, the Associated Press style recommends "mind your P's and Q's," but still omits the apostrophe in years.

Hot Hint

Indefinite pronouns <u>do</u> use an apostrophe to show possession. For example: *One's way of thinking, someone else's motorcar.*

26

Consider the Common Comma

Too often people profess that spelling, grammar, and punctuation don't really count that much in the world of online writing. "It's only e-mail," they proclaim.

Not true. The basic laws of the English language are just as important in an e-mail message as they are in a lofty letter. And what could be more basic than the common comma? Consider the following sentence, sans the helpful comma:

But if you don't take the time to use commas well your words string together making sentences difficult if not impossible to read understand and respond to.

Used properly, the seemingly simple comma can bring organization to your e-mails and meaning to your messages. Following are six situations is which a comma is called for.

#1: When you want the reader to take a brief pause. For example:

- *The cafeteria is serving better food, at least since the last time I went.*

Hot Hint

If you are writing an e-mail and you are not certain whether a comma is needed, try reading the sentence at normal speed as if there were no comma. Does it sound confusing? If it does, use it. If it doesn't, ditch it.

#2: Separating an aside that is not essential to the meaning of the sentence. For example:

- *I cleaned out all the files, which were too thick to fit in the drawer.*

In this sentence, all files were cleaned out and they were all too thick to fit in the drawer. However, by removing the comma, the meaning changes. For example:

- *I cleaned out all the files that were too thick to fit in the drawer.*

In that sentence, *only* the thick files were cleaned out.

#3: Replacing "and" when placed before a noun. For example, rather than writing:

- *The things I like about my job are my boss and my coworkers and my office and the things I get to do during the day.*

Replace the "ands" with commas:

- *The things I like about my job are my boss, my co-workers, my office, and the things I get to do during the day.*

#4: Separating a dependent clause from an independent clause—when the dependent clause comes first. For example:

- *After I cleaned the whiteboard, I was able to start the brainstorming session.*

The clause *after I cleaned the whiteboard* is dependent on the second clause.

However, if the independent clause comes first, a comma is not needed. For example:

- *I was able to start the brainstorming meeting after I cleaned the whiteboard.*

#5: Separating items on a list. For example:

- *My last order included pens, paper, rulers, chairs, and fly swatters.*

However, if the items in the list are long or contain a comma, use a semicolon to separate the items, and introduce the list with a colon. For example:

- *My last order included: pens, for marking the entry tickets; paper, for writing notes; rulers; chairs; and fly swatters.*

#6: To introduce a quote. For example:

- *I was surprised when I got to work and my boss said, "Good morning. Isn't it a beautiful day?"*

A Word About Colons

The colon is another small but useful tool in your online writing arsenal.

Here are the colon's key applications for e-mail.

- At the end of a salutation to a person you don't know well. For example, *Dear Mr. James:*
- To intrduce a logical consequence of a stated fact. For example, *I could only think of one thing: how to get home without a car.*
- To introduce dialogue. For example,

Manager: "Ben, thanks for helping with that delivery."

Ben: "No problem."

- To introduce a description, especially when parts of a set. For example, *There are three groups attending the meeting: marketing, finance, and production.*

27

Save Time With Contractions

In this no-time, gotta-run, get-to-the-bottom-line business world, the contraction is king. Contractions shorten a word by removing a letter (or a few) and placing an apostrophe in the empty spot. Here's a list of common contractions.

Phrase	Contraction
are not	aren't
cannot	can't
could not	couldn't
did not	didn't
does not	doesn't
do not	don't
had not	hadn't
has not	hasn't
have not	haven't
he would	he'd
he will	he'll
I am	I'm
I have	I've
I would	I'd

is not	isn't
it will	it'll
let us	let's
must not	mustn't
she is	she's
she will	she'll
should not	shouldn't
that is	that's
they are	they're
they have	they've
they will	they'll
we are	we're
we have	we've
we will	we'll
were not	weren't
what is	what's
who is	who's
would not	wouldn't
you are	you're
you have	you've
you will	you'll

A few contractions that aren't really contractions have reared their ugly heads. They are: *woulda, coulda, havta, shoulda, yaknow, gonna, gotta, wanna,* and *ain't*. Use them at your own peril.

28

Capitalize on Cue

Many eager beaver e-mailers feel it's easier and more efficient to type their messages in all lowercase. But with the rapid pace at which striking a keyboard has taken over putting pen to paper (think resumes, proposals, and reports), good business correspondence requires accurate capitalization. If you need some help sorting the big from the small, follow these basic guidelines.

The word *I*, as in me, myself, and I, is always capitalized. For example: "I love learning the rules of capitalization."

The first word of a sentence always begins with a capital. For example: "*She* is a terrific speller."

Days of the week are always in capital letters. For example: "I love *Monday*, *Wednesday*, and *Friday*—but *Thursdays* and *Tuesdays* are lousy."

The names of countries, cities, and specific locations are all capitalized. For example: "Jane visited *Paris*, *France*, where she watched the *Seine* from the *Left Bank*."

Hot Hint

The word *the* is not usually considered part of a place name and as such should be typed in lowercase. For example: *"He has not been to visit the Great Salt Lake."*

Hot Hint

Nonspecific locations are not capitalized. For example: "The *mountaintop*, the *beach*, the *backwoods*."

Languages are capitalized. For example: "Judy is so smart. She speaks *French*, *Spanish*, *English*, *Italian*, *Chinese*, and *Turkish*!"

Hot Hint

Language names used for common objects should not be capitalized. For example: "Keith loves to get french fries at the local bistro, then take a Spanish siesta and finally finish it all off with a turkish bath." (Spanish siesta uses capitalization because it is not a common object, but specific to Spain.)

Proper names of people and organizations are usually typed in the big letters. For example: "*Dr. Jack Smith* is president of *Smithco* and also the vice president of *Botswana*. His wife, *Sheri Dee Smith*, likes it there, but misses the small town in Minnesota where she grew up."

Hot Hint

Titles that come after a name should be lowercase. For example: "My friend Bill plans on running for *senator* of our state next year." Or, "Bob Jones is *mayor* of our town."

North, South, East, and West are capitalized when used as geographical areas: For example: "Jon and Janice met in the *West*."

Hot Hint

Whenever *north*, *south*, *east*, and *west* are used as directions, they should be in lowercase: For example: "Jon drove *east* to meet Janice, while the birds above their heads flew *south* for the winter."

Days of the week, holidays, and months of the year should all be capitalized. For example: "On *Friday*, *October* 31, it will be *Halloween*."

Hot Hint

When writing the name of the seasons, in general stick to the small letters. For example: "This *fall* I plan on taking a trip *south*." Capitalize if used in a title. For example: "I am planning on attending the *Fall 2009* football season."

The first word in a sentence of a quote is capitalized. For example: "Sharon spoke highly of Shannon. In fact, she said, '*Without* a doubt, Shannon is the best friend I have ever had.'"

The major words in a title (book, movie, magazine, song, painting) start with large letters. For example: "Julie enjoys the movie *The Sound of Music*, but loves the book *The Sound of Music: The Making of America's Favorite Movie*.

Hot Hint

Connecting words (*and, or, but, for*) and articles (*a, an, the*) are not written in caps unless they are the first word of the title. For example: "*The Elements of Style*."

Members of groups are capitalized. For example: "I am a *Democrat*, my husband is a *Republican*. But we both agree that the *San Francisco Giants* are the greatest baseball team around. We are also both long-time *Sierra Club* members."

Exercise

Take a look at the following paragraph and correct the 22 capitalization mistakes within.

jane just can't wait to go to italy in september and see the spanish steps. She has heard about them from her cousin in the western united states—mayor paula perkins. she first fell in love with the idea when she saw the movie roman holiday, with gregory peck and audrey hepburn. Now all she needs to do is learn to speak italian. "i'm going to start taking lessons right away," she tells her sister maggie, who lives in the southeast.

Correct Answers

Jane just can't wait to go to **I**taly in **S**eptember and see the **S**panish **S**teps. She has heard about them from her cousin in the **W**estern **U**nited **S**tates—**M**ayor **P**aula **P**erkins. **S**he first fell in love with the idea when she saw the movie ***Roman Holiday***, with **G**regory **P**eck and **A**udrey **H**epburn. Now all she needs to do is learn to speak **I**talian. "**I**'m going to start taking lessons right away," she tells her sister **M**aggie, who lives in the **S**outheast.

29

Use the Trusty Transition

When you want to create a bridge between one idea and the next, two sentences, a few words, or two paragraphs, use the trusty transition. Transitions are a handy helper for e-mail messages, because they keep the reader from getting lost in a plethora of paragraphs and swampland of sentences. Here are a few situations in which the transition can make your message flow more smoothly.

If you want to *make a point*, try these transitions:

I know how you feel, but the *first thing to remember is...*

I know how you feel, but *on the positive side...*

I know how you feel, but I just want *to point out...*

I know how you feel, and *with this in mind...*

I know how you feel, and *surprisingly enough...*

I know how you feel, but *to repeat my point...*

I know how you feel, but we *need to keep in mind...*

If you want to *conclude or summarize*, try these transitions:

We have closed the Jones account, *so, as a result...*

We have closed the Jones account; *therefore...*

We have closed the Jones account; *consequently...*

We have closed the Jones account, *so, in summary...*

We have closed the Jones account; *thus...*

We have closed the Jones account, *so, in short...*

If you want to *contrast* items, try these transitions:

I think we should go with the Foster Plan *as opposed to...*

I think we should go with the Foster Plan, but *even so...*

I think we should go with the Foster Plan, but *on the other hand...*

I think we should go with the Foster Plan, *otherwise...*

I think we should go with the Foster Plan, but *in the meantime...*

I think we should go with the Foster Plan *even though...*

If you want to *add information*, try these transitions:

The customer registered a complaint *along with...*

The customer registered a complaint *in addition to...*

The customer registered a complaint; *moreover...*

The customer registered a complaint *as well as...*

The customer registered a complaint, and *equally important...*

30

Master the Most Misspelled Words

Some words are just itching to be misspelled. They are often written incorrectly because they look as if they are spelled correctly! They will usually be caught by a spellchecker, but for those times when you are flying solo, without the aid of technology, here's a list of the top tricksters that can fool even the killer spellers among you.

Correct	Incorrect	Tip or Trick
Acceptable	Acceptible	If offered a table, take it!
Accidentally	Accidently	
Accommodate	Acomodate	It's big enough for two *c*s and two *m*s.
Acquire	Aquire	
Acquit	Aquit	
A lot	Alot	Two words is a lot more than one.
Amateur	Amature	Amateurs are not always mature.
Apparent	Aparent	
Argument	Arguement	The *e* lost the argument.
Atheist	Atheest	
Believe	Beleive	*I* before *e*, except after *c*.
Bellwether	Bellweather	Bells don't ring on a stormy day.
Calendar	Calender	
Category	Catagory	
Cemetery	Cemetary	
Changeable	Changable	
Collectible	Collectable	
Column	Columne	
Committed	Commited	I'm so committed I double my *t*.
Conscience	Consience	Be conscious of two *c*s, not one.

Correct	Incorrect	Tip or Trick
Conscientious	Consientious	
Conscious	Consious	
Consensus	Concensus	For consensus you don't need a census.
Daiquiri	Daiquri	
Definite	Definit	
Discipline	Dicipline	The *s* disciplines the *c*.
Drunkenness	Drunkeness	
Dumbbell	Dumbell	Dumb people don't ring a bell.
Embarrassment	Emabarassment	
Equipment	Equiptment	
Exercise	Excercise	
Exhilarate	Exilarate	
Exceed	Excede	
Existence	Existance	
Experience	Experiance	
Fiery	Firey	
Foreign	Foriegn	
Grateful	Greatful	Keep the *great* out of *grateful*.
Guarantee	Guarranty	
Harass	Harrass	Don't be harassed by two *r*s.
Height	Heighth	
Humorous	Humorus	It's funny how the *r* is between an *o* sandwich.

Correct	Incorrect	Tip or Trick
Ignorance	Ignorence	
Independent	Independant	
Indispensable	Indispensible	If you're able, you're indispensable.
Inoculate	Innoculate	
Intelligence	Intelligance	
Jewelry	Jewellery	
Judgment	Judgement	The judge decided to do away with the *e*.
Leisure	Liesure	
Liaison	Liason	It takes two *i*s to have a liaison.
License	Licence	You have the license to use both a *c* and an *s*.
Maneuver	Manuver	
Medieval	Medevil	
Millennium	Milennium	This word is big enough for two *l*s and two *n*s.
Mischievous	Mischievious	
Misspell	Mispell	
Neighbor	Nieghbor	
Noticeable	Noticable	
Occasionally	Ocasionaly	
Occurrence	Ocurrance	
Possession	Posession	I'm possessed with four *ss*.
Questionnaire	Questionaire	

Correct	Incorrect	Tip or Trick
Recommend	Recomend	I would recommend you put two *ms* in this word.
Referred	Refered	
Relevant	Relavant	
Separate	Seperate	
Sergeant	Sergent	
Threshold	Threshhold	
Tyranny	Tyrany	
Vacuum	Vacume	

31

Sharpen Your Spelling

If you've ever had a conversation with someone who has a piece of spinach stuck to his or her tooth, you know what a big distraction something so small can be. It's the same with misspelled words in an e-mail. No matter how well put together the prose, a spelling mistake can be distracting because it interrupts the reader's flow and diminishes your credibility. Consider the following example:

"We are verry excited about your perchase of our Little Farmer Composting Unit. We will be shipping the unit from our warehouse in the next few dys."

Even though the little farmer inside you may be excited about the delivery, the misspelled words might make you wonder whether the company will accurately process your order and even send it to the correct address.

Even though there are exceptions, knowing even these four basic rules of English spelling can help eliminate common errors.

Rule #1: *i* before *e*, except after *c*.

Example: Mischief, believe, field (*i* before *e*)

Example: Receive, conceit (except after *c*).

Exception: When it sounds like an *a*, as in *eight* or *freight*.

Rule #2: Drop the *e* before a suffix that starts with a vowel (*a*, *e*, *i*, *o*, *u*), but not before a suffix that begins with a consonant.

Example: love + ing = loving, row + ing = rowing (suffix begins with a vowel).

Example: displace + ment = displacement, like + ness = likeness (suffix begins with a consonant).

Exception: noticeable, truly.

*A suffix is a letter or group of letters added at the end of a word to form another word; for example, -ly in *briskly* or -ing in *caring*.

Rule #3: Change a final *y* to *i* before a suffix, unless the suffix begins with *i*.

Example: Supply + es = supplies, happy + ness = happiness (suffix does not begin with an i)

Example: play + ing = playing, study + ing = studying (suffix begins with an i).

Exception: obeyed.

Rule #4: Adding a prefix to a word does not change its spelling.

Example: Dis + interested = disinterested, un + necessary = unnecessary.

Typos Happen

Typos can happen to the nicest people—even those who won spelling bees in school. Contrary to popular belief, typos do not materialize the moment you hit the *send* button and your message is out in cyberspace with no possibility of a rewrite. Unfortunately, computer spellcheckers don't catch typos that morph into real words (wood instead of would, for example), so always take a moment to read through your e-mail again before you send it.

32

Don't Get Hung Up on Homophones

Homophones are words that sound the same, but are spelled differently and have different meanings. Technically, when misused, they're not misspelled—they're just the wrong version of the word. The classic example that catches millions of unsuspecting e-mail writers off guard every day is *here* (where you are) and *hear* (what your ears do). Spelling a word correctly requires knowing its correct meaning. To test your current level of homophone health, choose the right words to complete the following sentences.

1. Since Jane came down with the mumps, she has looked lumpy and _____.
   (pail/pale)
2. Bob is a man of _____; that's why they made him the high school_____.
   (principal/principle)

3. To Jennifer's delight, the ____of flowers wafted throughout the meadow.
(sent/scent)
4. Candy takes out her personalized ____ to write a thank-you note to Carl.
(stationery/stationary)
5. Even if the____outside is bad, I'm going,____you come or not.
(whether/weather)
6. Bill, can you put ____packages down over ____?
(there/their)
7. Sally, we are all going on break. Would you like to come ____?
(to/too)
8. Jennifer just ____she was right about that wall color—it was perfect.
(new/knew)
9. Carol decided to wear something____for her ____trip home.
(plane/plain)
10. Chaz was ____ with his chocolate, caramel-coated cashew phase, so he____them out.
(threw/through)

Answers

1. Since Jane came down with the mumps she looked lumpy and **pale.**
2. Bob is a man of **principle**, that's why they made him the high school **principal**.
3. To Jennifer's delight, the **scent** of flowers wafted throughout the meadow.
4. Candy takes out her personalized **stationery** to write a thank-you note to Carl.

5. Even if the **weather** outside is bad, I'm going, **whether** you come or not.
6. Bill, can you put **their** packages down over **there**?
7. Sally, we are all going on break. Would you like to come **too**?
8. Jennifer just **knew** she was right about that wall color—it was perfect.
9. Carol decided to wear something **plain** for her **plane** trip home.
10. Chaz was **through** with his chocolate, caramel-coated cashew phase, so he threw **them** out.

Word	Meaning	Word	Meaning
Advice	Opinion	Advise	To offer an opinion
Affect	To act upon something	Effect	A change
Compliment	Praise	Complement	To complete or perfect
Desert	The Sahara	Dessert	Plum pudding
Moral	Code of behavior	Morale	Mood, well-being
Principle	An ethical standard	Principal	High rank or money invested
Stationary	Not moving	Stationery	Writing supplies
Their	Relating to people	There	Indicating a place or thing
To	Direction or destination	Too	In addition or more of
Whether	Indicating a possibility of choice	Weather	Sun, wind, rain
Your	Belongs or relates to	You're	Contraction of "you are"

Word	Meaning	Word	Meaning
Site	A location	Sight	What you see
Threw	A fit, a ball, one's back out	Through	Movement
New	Recently made or created	Knew	Understood
Peace	Freedom from war or calm state of mind	Piece	Of cake, pie, pizza
Allowed	Given permission	Aloud	Can be heard
Higher	Placed above	Hire	To ______ an employee
Timber	Wood	Timbre	Voice tone or quality

When in doubt, check it out!

If you need to hone your homophones, you can find a large A to Z list at *www.homophone.com*.

33

Avoid the 10 Top E-Mail Mistakes

In the world of e-mail etiquette, almost every message contains a few mishaps and blunders. The following e-mail contains the 10 most common mistakes made. Read through the message and see if you can spot them all. We've listed the answers at the end, so resist the urge to cheat by peeking ahead.

Subject: Your procedure sucks!!
From: Jack B. Nimble
Date: Friday, Aug 11
To: Bill Melater
Cc: Doug Heelsin, Cal Oricounter, Carrie Mehome, Jack Thecarup, Foster Goodtimes, Bettina Urshirtonit

I am so tirred of having to deal with your outdated and stupid prosedures >:(Everytime ZI deal with your department it turns into a LOL situation. What do I have to do to get my adress chaned? I moved 6 months ago a you still haven't been able to update my records. I WORK IN THE SAME COMPANY AS YOU BUT YOU SEEM TO BE THE ENEMY!!!!!! My paycheck is still being forwarded from my old address this keeps me getting it late. Did you receve the form to have it deposited directly into my bank account? I don't think so. I sent you a fax with my bank account number but you've probably lost that X(Here it is again: #5866634792 If you did nothing has changed!! !!!!!! I want to pick up my paycheck personally from your office—is this possible. Until this whole fiasco is cleared up. When is it cut and ready to be picked up? GET BACK TO ME SOON!!

---

1. ______________________________
2. ______________________________
3. ______________________________
4. ______________________________
5. ______________________________
6. ______________________________

7. ______________________________
8. ______________________________
9. ______________________________
10. ______________________________

Answers

Mistake 1: Sloppy spelling, ghastly grammar, and poor punctuation.

This e-mail is difficult to read because of all the misspelled words and badly constructed sentences. The general carelessness of the message gives the receiver an instant negative impression of the sender, and concern about his or her credibility—which all can affect future correspondence.

Mistake 2: No salutation or signoff.

Don't start your e-mail with a description of a predicament or launch into the meat of your message. Instead, begin any e-mail (even one that is addressing a problem) with a friendly salutation. Just as important as a friendly greeting, a friendly closing is essential. Always end with a positive—*thank you, sincerely, best,* or another polite signoff.

Mistake 3: Divulges security-sensitive information.

E-mails are like newspapers lying around on a park bench—they can be picked up and viewed by anyone. Careful thought should be given before confidential information is written in an e-mail message. For example, the bank account number in this message might provide an unscrupulous person with information needed to wipe out the writer's bank account.

Mistake 4: No clear request.

The writer has asked so many different questions it's hard to know what he or she really wants the recipient to do. Does he or she want to pick up his or her paycheck, have it deposited electronically, or have it mailed to the correct address? To minimize confusion, make your requests easy to understand (and fulfill) by writing exactly what you want, and when you want it.

33

Mistake 5: Using all capital letters.

Capital letters are the online equivalent of shouting in someone's face, and have been know to start many a "flame war" such that the recipient (angered by the sender's rudeness) sends back an even nastier message...and on it goes. Only use capital letters for acronyms and proper spelling.

Mistake 6: Unclear subject line.

Most people give priority to opening e-mails with a clear and informative subject line. This message gives only a hint about what the e-mail is about, and is written rudely at that.

Mistake 7: Ambiguous acronyms.

Don't assume your readers are up to speed on all your in-house shorthand. Play it safe by staying away from uncommon abbreviations when dealing with clients. For example: LOL (laughing out loud) might be a well-known acronym to the under-40 crowd, but not everyone knows what it stands for.

Mistake 8: Obscure emoticons.

Emoticons are symbols that add expression to an e-mail, the most common being the smiley face :-) or the sad face :-(.

In our example, the author has also used >:(, which means angry, and X(, which means pouty. It's doubtful that many people outside of a few of the writer's close friends will know what these mean.

Mistake 9: Lack of important information.

The writer of this e-mail would get what he or she wants much faster if he or she supplied the recipient with more important information and less attitude. For example, including specific dates when requests were made would make it easier for the reader to research and respond to the issue.

Mistake 10: Unprofessional tone.

This message, from the very first line, has a rude and unpleasant tone. Remember the old saying, "You catch more flies with honey than you do with vinegar." If you have a sensitive problem to deal with in your e-mail, don't make the message accusatory or hostile in nature. The reader will immediately be put on the defensive, making a helpful response unlikely.

34

Get a Grip on the Jargon

Technology in general, and e-mail in particular, has a whole slew of crazy words, abbreviations, and acronyms that can make a relatively simple process—such as setting up your new e-mail account—complicated and frustrating. Following is a list of common terms and what they mean to the average e-mail user.

Archive. A way of compressing and storing e-mails that takes them out of your e-mail program and places them in a separate, less readily accessible file. If you notice that it's taking longer and longer to download new messages, it's probably because you have too many old messages taking up memory space. Archiving past e-mails frees up space and puts the zip back in your inbox.

ASCII. American Standard Code for Information Interchange—or, a set of codes based on the English alphabet. President Lyndon B. Johnson, in 1968, officially announced that all computers purchased by the United States federal government support ASCII. The result being that ASCII files are the basis for most text characters, which means they are readable by any computer.

Autoresponder. A message that you create for automatically replying to e-mails that arrive in your inbox. Autoresponders are useful for letting others know you are going to be unavailable and away from your e-mail. For example, when going on vacation, an autoresponder you create provides the reader with the dates you will be out and who to contact in case of an emergency. Another use is to let a client know you have received his or her question or problem, and will get back to him or her within a given period of time.

BCC. Blind carbon copy is a throwback to the typewriter days, when duplication of a document meant placing carbon paper between two sheets of paper. "Blind" means that the recipients who are copied on the e-mail cannot see each other's names when they receive the message. This is a useful tool when you don't want to make public the names of all the recipients on the list.

Hot Hint

Some programs reveal the names of your BCC list when the recipient responds to your e-mail by selecting "reply all." Test this out before sending sensitive information.

Bounced message. This is an e-mail that is returned to you because it cannot be delivered to the recipient's mailbox. Bounced e-mails are usually the result of an incorrect e-mail address or a full mailbox on the other end.

Hot Hint

In certain cases, a full mailbox will not result in a bounced message notification. This means that neither you nor the other person knows that the message wasn't received or read. Avoid this by programming your e-mail client to empty your mailbox regularly.

Browser. A program that allows you to view Web pages. Popular browsers include Apple Safari, Microsoft Internet Explorer, and Mozilla Firefox.

CC. Carbon copy. Unlike blind copies, inserting addresses in the CC field means that the e-mail addresses of all those copied on it can be viewed by the recipient.

Distribution list. A set of e-mail addresses that are grouped together under one name. Whenever you click on the designated distribution list, all the names and e-mail addresses on that list are entered in the "To" field. For example, if you regularly send e-mails to everyone in the accounting department, dragging their names and addresses to a distribution list called "Accounting" would allow you to send e-mails to everyone, simply by selecting the "Accounting" distribution list as the party the e-mail should be sent to.

Encryption. A method for making an e-mail message unreadable to unauthorized people. Only the person who has the key for decoding the message (decryption) can read it.

Firewall. This is an appliance or software that inspects all the network traffic that passes through it and prohibits the entry of any unauthorized users.

Host. Any computer that has two-way access to any other computers on the network. For example, when you type a Web address into your browser, the computer—or server—that delivers those pages is a host. Often, within a company network, the host computer means a more powerful device that provides centralized services to its "clients"—less capable computers—such as data files, e-mail processing, and software applications.

IMAP. Internet message access protocol. This is a method for retrieving e-mail messages stored on mail servers. It can be accessed by multiple machines, including laptops, desktop computers, and PDAs, without the need to transfer the messages back and forth between machines.

Intranet. A private computer network within an organization for securely sharing information with and between employees.

IP address. Internet protocol address. This is a series of numbers, such as 111.22.345.67, that is unique to each computer. When using e-mail or the Web, Internet service providers (ISPs) would provide a dedicated IP address to each user accessing the system. These are called *static IP addresses*. However, the pool of static IP addresses was too small to deal with increased usage of the Internet, and ISPs now issue IP addresses in a dynamic fashion from a pool. These are called *dynamic IP addresses*.

MIME. Multipurpose Internet mail extension. This is a standard that allows audio, video, and graphics files, for example, to be sent over the Internet. If your e-mail recipients have MIME-compliant e-mail programs (most are), swapping attachments is easy and automatic.

POP. Post office protocol; a protocol for retrieving messages from an e-mail server. Older than the IMAP protocol, POP is used primarily by e-mail programs that reside in your computer rather than on the Web, such as Microsoft Outlook and Apple Mail.

SMTP. Simple mail transfer protocol; a protocol for sending messages from one server to another. When configuring your e-mail application you will need to specify your SMTP server for outgoing messages.

TCP/IP. Transmission control protocol/Internet protocol. This is the basic communication language of the Internet. When you have direct access to the Internet, your computer is provided with a copy of the TCP/IP program, as is every other computer that you send messages to or get information from.

Thread. A series of related e-mails that form an ongoing e-mail conversation.

URL. Uniform resource locator; the global address of individual sites, pages, and resources on the Web. You can get to a Website by entering the URL (such as *www.whatever.com*) of its home page in your Web browser's address line.

35

Don't Fan the Flames

A *flame* is an e-mail message that uses negative and not-so-nice language to forcefully deliver an inflammatory opinion or point of view. Flaming is the online version of face-to-face conflict, such that one person makes a provocative remark and the other immediately fires a zinger back, and so on. However, the online medium, unlike the real world, offers anonymity without the fear of embarrassment or physical aggression, so flaming is more common because there's less personal risk to life and limb.

One single flame can start a "flame war" such that an ongoing back-and-forth rally of insults builds to a deafening crescendo. Many flames are started with the use of ALL CAPITAL LETTERS—the e-mail equivalent of screaming. Imagine receiving this message in your mailbox.

Subject: I'm really PO'd
From: Barbi
Date: Friday, June 13
To: Pamela

WHAT WERE YOU THINKING? Was it to much too ask that you cover my phone yesterday?! YOU SAID YOU WOULD—but I now know you didn't. That was very THOUGHTLESS and has caused me a lot of grief today.

Your buttons have been pressed and you are ready to do some flaming of your own—right back at Barbi! Your response might look like this:

Subject: Re: I'm really PO'd
From: Pamela
Date: Friday, June 13
To: Barbi

I'VE HAD ENOUGH OF YOUR PATHETIC WHINING. You take so much time off, I can't answer you phone all day long. I have my own to answer. Perhaps you should look for another job—one where you don't have to be responsible for anything!

Barbi, wanting the last word, responds to this e-mail with more uppercase upper cuts, and so it goes until the flame loses its heat and turns to ashes—with the situation unresolved and the coworker relationship damaged.

If you are ever flamed, try to avoid the knee-jerk reaction to fight back and fire off an equally poisonous message of your own. Instead of fanning the flames, allow them to die quickly by either not responding, or, if it is necessary to respond, waiting until you are calm and collected. Here is the message that Pamela might have sent if she had resisted the urge to fire back so fiercely:

Subject: Re: I'm really PO'd
From: Pamela
Date: Friday, June 13
To: Barbi

Barbi:I got your message. I wanted to explain that I was getting your phone yesterday until I got very busy and was unable to. We have to work together so I want to resolve this. When can we talk by phone or in person?

Pamela

Baiters

Baiters are people who deliberately try to elicit strong feelings from others by posting negative and inflammatory comments on Internet forums. They target specific groups and say anything (whether it makes sense or not) to have prominent forum members embarrass themselves by flaming back—behavior that is uncharacteristic of the person and consequently shocking to other members of the forum.

36

Nix the Negative Filters

What are some of the labels (in the privacy of your own mind) that you give your difficult customers and coworkers? Some common ones that float around the workplace include *stupid*, *rude*, *jerk*, *clueless*, *loser*, *creep*, *liar*, and all those with an R rating that we can't put in print.

The dark side of rose-colored glasses, these labels are usually the result of behaviors you see in others, judge to be bad, and then brand in a negative way. For example, imagine you work with a colleague who often has a hard time remembering instructions. Because of this periodic forgetfulness, you've labeled him or her as *stupid*, and whenever you work together, without realizing it, you listen to everything he or she says through that filter. In fact, you mostly hear the things he or she says as a *reinforcement* of that filter.

Similarly, when you talk back to this person, you speak to him or her through the same filter, and, without ever saying, "Hey you're not too bright!" your tone clearly conveys what you're thinking.

Negative filters are especially dangerous when it comes to writing e-mails, because the lack of body language and tone of voice already leaves the medium wide open to misinterpretation. Consider the following excerpt from an actual e-mail.

"...This is precisely the situation I was trying to avoid, when I asked you, very clearly, to whom I should refer things when you were out. You were so certain that there would not be a problem. I kept pressing you to make sure that someone else was backing you up. And what happened? Exactly the thing I asked you to address. You left no indication you were out of the office. What would that have taken? An extra 60 seconds at most?"

How would you feel if you received this e-mail? Filled with the joy of life, or ready for a fight? Perhaps without realizing it, the sender of this e-mail has conveyed a negative filter—that he or she thinks the recipient is stupid. Phrases such as: "when I asked you, very clearly," and "what would that have taken" carry an unspoken yet clearly implied tone of superiority, and even arrogance.

And it wouldn't end there. Negative filters breed more negative filters; you read the e-mail, dislike the tone of the sender, and write your reply now looking through your own filter.

E-mail conversations such as this often spiral downward very quickly, with both parties firing shots at one another rather than working together to resolve whatever issue is on the table.

The simplest way to avoid a negative filter in an e-mail is to read it through before you send it and ask yourself, how would I feel if I received this e-mail? If you don't like the answer you get, rewrite it until you do.

37

Beware Obscure Emoticons

Emoticons are symbols that add an emotional touch to online messages. The most common is a colon followed by hyphen and a right parenthesis. In short, a smiley face: :-)

For example, imagine reading the following e-mail message from an acquaintance: "I appreciated being invited to sit in on the monthly managers' meeting this morning. I couldn't figure who was running the meeting—you or them."

The message could easily be interpreted as a critical comment about how you facilitated the meeting. Now let's add a smiley: "I appreciated being invited to sit in on the monthly managers' meeting this morning. I couldn't figure who was running the meeting—you or them. :-)"

The tone is immediately different. The emoticon clarifies that this is a tongue-in-cheek remark, and removes any misunderstanding.

The use of shorthand to convey feelings in written messages goes back as far as the 1850s, when the number 73 signified "love and kisses" in Morse code. Today there are dozens of different emoticons—maybe too many—that can spice up your texts, e-mails, and instant messages.

Hot Hint

Use emoticons sparingly, if at all, in your important e-mail communications, because they can appear unprofessional to some people. They are much more suited to texting and instant messaging, where messages are usually casual and brief.

The smiley face is recognized by everyone, but there are many other emoticons that are so creative they can be hard to decipher. In general we don't recommend the use of these little symbols because they can lead to confusion. However, if you need to decode an e-mail you receive, the following list might prove useful. Use the space on the right to jot down your interpretation.

37

	Emoticon	Meaning
1.	>:(	
2.	@}->—	
3.	@:^)	
4.	l:*)	
5.	(( )):**	
6.	^5	
7.	|-O	
8.	’-)	
9.	\~/	
10.	@@@@:-)	
11.	}{	
12.	$-)	

1. Angry 2. Rose 3. Elvis 4. Drunk 5. Hugs and kisses 6. High five 7. Yawning 8. Winking 9. Glass is full 10. Marge Simpson 11. Face to face 12. Lottery winner.

On the Side or Straight Up?

Most Western emoticons are written sideways. In other words, you have to tilt your head to see their meaning. In Japanese, emoticons have taken a whole different path; they are read horizontally, and this opens up a whole new world of emoticon madness. For example:

(@_@) = Dizzy

(~_^) = Wink

(o|o) = Surprised

(=^_^=) = Cat

{{ (>_<) }} = Freezing cold

38

Sort Through Spam

Just in case you have been in a cave (without a wi-fi connection) for the past decade, spam is the unwanted, unsolicited e-mail everyone receives in their inbox—day in and day out. Spammers (those who spam) send bulk mailings indiscriminately to millions of e-mail users, the result being that inappropriate and unwanted messages (*Jim Johnson would you like a bigger...)* show up in your mailbox at work or at home. Only after sorting through seedy listings for pornography, gambling, organ enlargement, and an array of pharmaceuticals can you get to your legitimate messages.

Spam seems to be a necessary evil of having an e-mail account, and conservative estimates suggest that it makes up about 85 percent of the messages sent throughout the world each day. The United States is the biggest culprit by far, sending about 28 percent of all spam, according to a 2007 analysis by SophosLabs. In second place is South Korea (they send 5.2 percent) followed closely by China at 4.9 percent.

Why bother? You may ask, why do spammers bother? Does anyone actually fall for any of those pathetic messages? Well, Economy 101 (and Greed 102) tells us that spam would disappear overnight if someone, somewhere wasn't making a buck or two. Apparently, a small percentage of people *do* fall for spam, and this is all it takes, because spammers have almost no operating costs, and entry into the "business" requires no start-up capital. A tiny return on millions of e-mails quickly adds up and turns into profit. Although spam is illegal in the United States, spammers usually outsource parts of their operation to countries where there is little chance of legal action.

The cost of spam is borne by us, the receivers—not the senders. According to a 2007 report by the California Legislature, U.S. companies spent $13 billion in lost productivity and the technology and manpower required to manage unwanted messages. Small businesses also bear the burden, requiring special software and spending extra man hours to capture genuine messages and filter out the unwanted. The more spam-filtering software improves, the sneakier and more sophisticated the spammers become.

How do they find my mailbox? Spammers have a few different ways of "harvesting" your address. The simplest is that one spammer simply purchases a list from another. Your address was probably collected, originally, from a harvesting bot—software that trawls the Web looking for e-mail addresses posted on Web pages. Regardless of the spammers' methods for getting you on their pesky lists, your challenge is to find a way to keep them at bay and out of your mailbox.

What can I do about it? Many users find that Web-based e-mail accounts, such as Google's Gmail, do an efficient job of screening out spam and "learning" (from your actions) which messages to ditch in the future.

If you use an e-mail client such as Microsoft Entourage or Apple Mail, the chances are that they are only doing a so-so job of protecting you from spam because the spammers improve their technology faster than your program can learn. To beef up your spam filtering, use a third-party software such as SpamEater Pro for Windows or SpamSieve for the Mac.

Spam, Spam, Spam, Spam!

The word *spam* comes from a 1970 BBC television comedy series called *Monty Python's Flying Circus*. One sketch from the show takes place in a café where everything on the menu comes with Spam, the canned meat product. A Viking chorus (this will only make sense if you've seen any Monty Python comedy) sing "Spam, Spam, Spam, Spam, wonderful Spam..." and so on, drowning out any other dialogue. In the 1980s, during the early days of electronic bulletin boards, abusive members would type the word "spam" over and over to scroll other users' postings off the screen. This was the birth of spamming.

39

Avoid Phishing Like the Plague

Phishing is an illegal process for trying to get you to divulge your personal information, such as passwords, usernames, credit card numbers, bank account information, and Social Security numbers. In order to fool you, the e-mails appear to be coming from services to which you subscribe, such as PayPal, Youtube, Facebook, eBay, or your bank. The message provides a link to a Website that looks, feels, and smells just like the real thing; even experts have a problem knowing the difference.

Once on the Web page you are asked to enter personal information in order to log in and "verify" your identity—except that the information is captured for illicit purposes. Successful phishing trips often result in financial loss for the innocent parties and a long, exasperating process of reestablishing credibility and security with the accounts that were breached.

Knowing what to look for. Here are some ways to distinguish between a genuine and fraudulent message.

1. Recognize commonly used phishing phrases. For example, if you receive an e-mail that says any of the following phrases, assume that it is a scam, and delete the message.

"We suspect an unauthorized transaction on your account. To ensure that your account is not compromised, please click the link below and confirm your identity."

"If you don't respond within 48 hours, your account will be closed."

"During our regular verification of accounts, we couldn't verify your information. Please click here to update and verify your information."

2. Look for bad spelling or grammar. Because many phishing scams originate in non-English-speaking countries, awkward language and misspelled words tell you that all is not what it seems.
3. Do they use a generic greeting? Phishing messages will not use information that is specific to your account. For example, a genuine message from eBay will begin with a greeting that includes your username. A phishing e-mail will begin with a non-specific greeting such as *Dear Valued Customer.*
4. Is there an attachment from an unverified source? If there is, don't click on it. Doing so can release malware (malicious software that gets into your computer and does bad things) that invisibly finds and transmits security-sensitive information from your computer to theirs.

Anti-phishing software. Adding anti-spam software to your computer adds another level of security beyond that of your personal inspection of possible scam sites. Usually, this software, once installed, shows up in the toolbar of your Web browser. When you go to a possible phishing Web page, the toolbar alerts you to the hosting location (for example, a genuine PayPal site would not be hosted in, say, Korea), the name of the organization hosting the site, a risk rating, and any deceptive characters designed to hide the real URL. If you use anti-phishing software, be sure to update regularly so that your software is current with the latest fraudulent developments of the scammers.

Follow the Money

According to a survey conducted by the Gartner Group, 3.6 million adults lost $3.2 billion in 2007, a 200 percent increase over 2005 statistics. Who's making the money on these fraudulent sites? Although it's hard to find the culprits, who hide their tracks with technological smoke screens, there have been two notable arrests.

In 2005, Valdir Paulo de Almeida was arrested in Brazil for heading up one of the largest phishing crime rings. His organization made between $18 million and $37 million during a two-year period. In 2006, the Japanese authorities arrested a team of eight phishing criminals who made a quick $870,000.

40

Beef Up Your E-Mail Security

The convenience of e-mail and instant messaging can easily eclipse good judgment and cause security issues. Understanding that an online note can be forwarded to the entire world still doesn't stop some people from abusing the medium. Examples of security blunders are continually hitting the headlines.

- In 2006, Mark Foley, Republican congressman of Florida, resigned because of inappropriate e-mails and IMs sent to congressional pages in 2005.
- Harry Stonecipher, Boeing CEO, resigned after e-mail love letters surfaced that had been sent to his Boeing VP mistress.
- In 2003, the Federal Energy Regulatory Committee (FERC) investigating the Enron scandal posted 1.6

> million private employee e-mails alongside Enron's business records for anyone to see. Employee's Social Security numbers, bank information, performance reviews, and other personal information was all there, with senders' and receivers' names attached! Eventually, FERC removed the e-mails with SS numbers, but not before millions of people—including identity thieves—had viewed them.

To avoid such embarrassments yourself, follow this list of security guidelines.

E-mail is NEVER private. A message is like a postcard, readable by everyone who has a computer. If you forward a message to 10 people, and they, in turn, forward it to 10 people, and so on for another three layers, in a very short time 100,000 people will have the e-mail in their inbox.

Blind copies can sometimes see. If you send a message to several people and place the names in the BCC window, don't assume that those names are hidden from others. For example, if you receive a message that has BCC attachments and then hit the "reply all" button, all the hidden recipients will show up in your "send to" window—as plain as day! To avoid this, send a separate e-mail to each individual person.

The Nigerian lawyer is not your friend. As convincing as it may appear (and as much as you may want to believe it), the lawyer that wants to dump $3 million in your lap because of a long-lost heir, is a scam. Assume the worst when it comes to winning the lotto, helping a Hong Kong businessman with a (well-rewarded) small financial favor, or personal invitations from Russian wanna-be brides.

Know when to use the phone. Regardless of the situation, you can seriously breach your own security by writing your bank account information, passwords, Social Security numbers, or credit card numbers in an e-mail. No matter how necessary or convenient it might seem, and no matter how trustworthy the recipient, the information might still get into the wrong hands. Always use the phone for conveying such personal information.

Keep it decent. Don't send off-color jokes, discriminatory remarks, sexually explicit messages, or rude comments via e-mail.

What you say can be used against you in a court of law. Unlikely? About 15 percent of companies battle lawsuits brought about by bad messages, with a similar percentage of e-mails from each company being subpoenaed for evidence.

Follow the policy. Know what your company's e-mail policy says, and follow it. You can be fired for not following e-mail policy—claiming "I never knew" is no defense.

41

Set Up a Responsible Rant

Whereas flaming may be an e-mail etiquette no-no, expressing your frustration and venting—to a safe source—is not. When done responsibly, an e-mail vent can help you let off steam when you're upset about something. If you ever need to vent in an e-mail or online discussion group—and you don't want anyone to take it personally—try using rant markers. The words "Begin Rant" and "End Rant" act as parentheses, marking the beginning and end of the get-it-off-your-chest section. For example:

Subject: Our office
From: Conan Hunak
Date: Friday, May 17
To: Operations Manager

Dear David:

I went over to the California office last week and couldn't believe how different it was from our office.

They had new office furniture, clean carpets, an attractive lobby, and free breakfast cereal. Free!

Begin Rant:

I have to say, by comparison, our office is dumpy!

We've got dingy paint, stained carpets, and a lobby that looks like it has not been redecorated since 1967.

We need to move to a new building or redo this place!

End Rant.

Anyway, I had a good time in California, and, as you can tell, it really got me thinking about where we work and what we can do to have a better work environment.

Best,

Conan

The intention of a responsible rant is to express strong feelings without deliberately upsetting, shocking, or insulting anybody—the opposite of what a flame does.

Hot Hint

Keep in mind that any e-mail has the potential to be accessed by any person, so if you would not want your message read by everyone and anyone, think twice before putting your woes in writing.

42

Keep Cultural Differences in Mind

Because the rules of business and social etiquette vary around the world, it is with good reason that companies send employees who will be traveling overseas to cultural sensitivity and diversity classes. Although you may not be literally taking a meeting in Manila or closing a deal in Cairo, e-mail lets you travel around the world from the comfort of your own desk.

You can create faster rapport and keep out of trouble if you make an attempt to adapt your e-mail style to the cultural rules of the person with whom you are communicating. As with all cultural styles, there are general guidelines to keep in mind, but specific exceptions to every rule. Here are just a few examples.

United States. The national need to be productive almost guarantees e-mails that are business-focused and aimed at moving matters forward. Rarely will a business e-mail to an associate stray into personal territory and mention family or other non-work-related subjects.

Hot Hint

When e-mailing within the United States, start with a pleasantry such as *I hope you are well*, and then quickly move to the subject at hand. Make direct, clear requests, and, if it is a new relationship, keep humor to a minimum—it can be misinterpreted, and backfire!

United Kingdom. Brits are less verbose than Americans, often using language more precisely with less repetition. Referencing family and personal life is not unusual, especially if the writer has a long relationship with the reader. Watch out for dry British humor, often snuck into a message where you least expect it. Tongue in cheek is their specialty.

Hot Hint

Start your message formally, and, depending on your relationship with the recipient, feel free to mention family and leisure topics toward the end of the e-mail. Humor is okay as long as it is connected with the subject of the message.

Germany, Switzerland, Austria. Many European countries tend toward the formal, and requests can come out sounding like demands.

They aren't, but may sound like it. For example, in a business e-mail, *You must get back to me by the end of the week* really means *please get back to me by the end of the week*. Likewise, short, curt sentences are a function of translation and should not be considered rude or abrasive.

Hot Hint

Keep your e-mail formal and short. Keep sentences in a logical order, but don't go into too much detail unless necessary. Use the recipient's last name unless you have a long, ongoing relationship. Steer clear of humor.

Japan. Not surprisingly, the Japanese e-mail style is very polite. For example, it's not unusual to be addressed as Mr. Smith, even after several interactions. Unlike the United States, Japanese e-mails will rarely make direct requests.

Hot Hint

Use a logical sentence structure and keep the message brief. Rather than making a direct request, such as *"We want you to deliver the reactor by August of next year,"* say, *"We are hoping for delivery next year. Do you think this will be possible?"*

Italy. Italians adore conversation. It's a national pastime. E-mails, although formal in style, are often warm and chatty. As in their face-to-face communications, Italians' e-mail messages can be long, with no pressing need to make a point or produce quick results. Family and personal life topics can be introduced once a relationship has been established.

Hot Hint

Don't be in a hurry to produce results when e-mailing Italians. Take your time to build a relationship and avoid situations that create undue pressure—such as a sales proposition in which decisions need to be made quickly.

43

Create an E-Mail Policy

E-mail has an immediacy and convenience that can make it seem less substantial and serious than information printed on paper. Because of its informal nature, employees will often type things in an e-mail that they would never dream of writing in a letter or memo. Too often this casual approach proves to be a recipe for disaster.

According to the 2007 Electronic Monitoring & Surveillance Survey conducted by the American Management Institute, almost a third of employers have fired workers for:

- Breach of confidentiality in e-mail—22%.
- Excessive personal use of e-mail—26%.
- Inappropriate or offensive language used in e-mails—62%.
- Violation of company e-mail policy—64%.
- Viewing, downloading, or uploading inappropriate/offensive content—84%.

Remember, e-mails are a permanent record of communication that can be saved, copied, forwarded, and printed. And if inappropriate messages are sent, a return address will identify them as originating from the employer's company.

Imagine the problems that could arise from an employee's personal political opinion being forwarded and publicly posted as your organization's official policy!

Other risks involve sending messages that contain copyrighted, confidential, or defamatory information that can be used against your business in a court of law. Several recent newspaper headlines highlight how carelessness with e-mail content can have a devastating impact on both the individual and one's corporation.

To avoid lawsuits and the expensive process of e-discovery, more and more companies are creating and implementing an official e-mail policy. Areas to be covered include:

- Your right as an employer to monitor and randomly check the content of e-mails sent and received on company equipment without prior notice to the employee.
- The conditions under which your company can access employees' e-mail messages.
- Guidelines regarding what is acceptable to include in e-mail communications.
- Guidelines regarding what is unacceptable in e-mail communications.
- Your company's e-mail backup and retention policy.
- How the organization will respond to noncompliance with the stated e-mail policy.

Reinforce the Message

Research shows that 80 percent of organizations are doing a good job of informing employees about their Internet usage policy by including the information as part of employee orientation. The problem is retention. To make the information stick, continually reinforce the e-mail policy by including it in newsletters, memos, and ongoing in-house training efforts.

44

Write an E-Mail Policy

A well-written and seriously enforced e-mail policy can help you reduce the risk of litigation. By informing your staff of what is permissible to communicate via e-mail and what is not, you reduce the chances of becoming one of the 24 percent of employers who have had their e-mail messages subpoenaed by courts and regulators. Your legal advisors, especially those who specialize in electronic communications, are the final authority on drafting an e-mail policy that is right for your organization. However, you can begin the process by thinking about the following questions:

- What are the acceptable uses of e-mail within your organization as they relate to:
  - Communicating with clients.
  - Communicating with other employees.
  - Communicating with all other business contacts.
  - Password protection, or encryption.
  - Confidential and copyrighted information that is to be sent electronically.
  - Scanning incoming e-mails and attachments for viruses.
- What are unacceptable uses of e-mail within your organization as they relate to:
  - Transmitting spam.
  - Sending unprotected messages that contain personal employee information or confidential company material.
  - Sending messages that contain fraudulent or offensive material.
  - Using e-mail for purposes that are illegal or unethical.
  - Forwarding chain letters.
  - Personal business.
  - Disseminating, viewing, or storing commercial or personal advertisements, solicitations, promotions, or any other unauthorized materials.

44

- What are standard mailbox management practices?
  - Deleting non-work related e-mails, once read.
  - Deleting work-related messages that are not required for reference, legal reasons, or in-house retention policies.
  - Setting up folders for organizing and systematizing the filing of retained documents.
- What are unacceptable mailbox practices?
  - Saving files that are not needed.
  - Using server space by storing personal messages in folders.
  - Sending large files that take a long time to download, create storage problems, and may be too big for the recipient's mailbox.
  - Storing important files in areas that are routinely purged by IT.

General Company Internet Usage Policies

To get an idea of the types of statements that make up an e-mail policy, check out the following samples.

Occasional limited and appropriate personal use of the computer is permitted if such use does not interfere with the user's or any other employee's job performance; have an undue effect on the computer or company network's performance; or violate any other policies, provisions, guidelines, or standards of our policy.

All electronic communications created, sent, or received through company servers are considered the property of the company and may be regarded as public information. We reserve the right to access the contents of any messages, for good reason, by legal counsel.

All communications sent or received using company computers can be disclosed to law enforcement or other third parties without prior consent of the sender or the receiver.

45

Brainstorm Possible Problem Causes

In today's global business environment, the luxury of sitting around a table to discuss and solve a problem is often geographically unrealistic. If you have team members in different locations, but are keen to use the group dynamic to solve problems, you can start by using the power of e-mail to brainstorm the possible causes of a problem.

The first step is to determine the group of individuals who should participate in the problem-solving process. It's best to select people who have a hands-on relationship with the problem and/or have useful knowledge to contribute. Once the group is selected (between four and 10 people works best), publish a simple, clear description of the problem and send it to all team members.

Hot Hint

Be careful not to state the problem as a solution. For example, say, *"Our fresh donut supply runs out before noon,"* rather than *"We need more donuts."*

Explain in your message that this is a brainstorming process, and encourage everyone to write down as many causes as they see fit. For those concerned about getting to solutions, let them know that these potential causes will be evaluated and whittled down in the next step. For example:

Subject: Donut Problem
From: Howard Uno
Date: Oct 6
To: Donut Team

Dear Team:

I would like to get your input regarding a problem that we've all been experiencing: A serious shortage of donuts every morning. Before we go about trying to solve this problem, I'd like to find out from each of you what you believe are the causes of this problem. I am open to hearing all of your ideas, so don't hold back. Please write down your thoughts and get them to me before noon on Wednesday. I will send you a list of what the group came up with on Monday morning. Please keep in mind that the purpose of this first step is to brainstorm causes, not evaluate them. We will do that later. Just as a reminder, brainstorming is a technique designed to get as many different ideas as possible generated about a specific subject. The goal here is to throw on the table whatever you think may be a contributing factor to our pastry problem.

Thanks,
Howie

46

Evaluate Possible Problem Causes

Once you have received the group's e-mails containing their ideas about what the problem's causes are, cut and paste the possible causes into a new e-mail that you send to the problem-solving team. Everyone on the team will see all the input. This is the online equivalent of brainstorming on a flip chart in a face-to-face meeting.

Ask each team member to review the possible causes listed, evaluate them, and come up with the one or two causes that they feel are at the heart of the problem. For example:

Subject: Donut Problem Causes
From: Howard Uno
Date: Oct 12
To: Donut Team

Dear Team:

Thank you for all your great input. Here are the main causes the group came up with: (1) Someone is eating more than his or her fair share. (2) The donuts are smaller than they used to be—50 donuts now is equal to about 35 donuts a year ago. (3) Someone is secretly bagging them up and feeding them to the ducks at lunchtime. (4) People are taking the donuts home to their family and friends. (5) We are ordering less donuts than we used to. (6) More people are offering vendors and clients donuts. Please consider these possible causes and let me know within the next two days which one or two, in your opinion, is the real cause of the problem. Some questions to think about include: What percentage of the problem will be solved if this cause is fixed? Is there a cause, creating this cause we are overlooking? Is this cause intermittent or constant?

Thanks,
Howie

47

Brainstorm Possible Problem Solutions

Once your team members have gotten back to you with their narrowed-down list of problem causes, the next step is to brainstorm possible solutions. Begin the process by pasting the responses in a new e-mail and send it to each member. For example:

Subject: Root Donut Problem Cause
From: Howard Uno
Date: Oct 15
To: Donut Team

Dear Team:

Thanks for your responses. There was a lot of agreement about the real, root cause of our donut problem. It was: The donuts are smaller than they used to be—50 donuts now is equal to about 35 donuts a year ago.Now that we have consensus on the cause, I want your input about what to do about it. Yes, we could buy more donuts, but I am interested to know if you have any other ideas. Again, the idea here is to brainstorm, so please send me as many ideas as you can think of—even if they seem somewhat off the wall. Please send me your ideas for solving this problem by end of day Wednesday.

Thanks,
Howie

48

Evaluate and Agree on the Problem Solution

Having gathered all the group members' suggested solutions, cut and paste their ideas into a new e-mail that you send to the problem-solving team. For example:

Subject: Donut Problem Solutions
From: Howard Uno
Date: Oct 17To: Donut Team

Dear Team:

What great responses you gave as to how we should solve the donut problem! Here is what you said:

1. Buy more donuts.
2. Wean ourselves off of donuts by replacing them with carrot and celery sticks one day a week.
3. Ration donuts based on body weight. Those who weigh more get less, and vice versa.
4. Change donut vendors so that we get full-size donuts—maybe at a better price.
5. Hold a weekly contest: whoever eats the fewest donuts gets to come in 30 minutes later on Fridays.

Please look these potential solutions over and let me know—by noon Friday please—which one you think will work the best. As you evaluate these potential solutions, please keep the following in mind. - Is this a solution our team can implement? - What will the short-term and long-term impact of this solution be? - Is this soulution relatively low cost? - Do we have the resources currently available to solve this problem? - Is this a solution management will buy into?

Thanks,
Howie

— —

Once you have received input from the team regarding what they think is the best solution, send an e-mail that notifies everyone of the most popular solution. For example:

Subject: Donut Problem Solution
From: Howard Uno
Date: Oct 20
To: Donut Team

Dear Team:

Thanks for your responses. Your solution to the donut problem is: Wean ourselves off of donuts by replacing them with carrot and celery sticks one day a week. Also, another popular solution is: Hold a weekly contest: whoever eats the fewest donuts gets to come in 30 minutes later on Fridays. I see no reason why we can't adopt both of these ideas. It will save us money—and, more importantly, keep us healthy.I will set up an action plan and forward you the details as soon as I've worked them out. Thank you for your great work on this!

Best,
Howie

What problems could you solve? What are some of the problems that you could work on using this e-mail problem-solving technique? For the best outcome, choose problems that you have a good deal of control over. Problems that lay outside your immediate sphere of influence will be harder to implement—no matter how good the solution.

49

Find an E-Mail Marketing Service

As much as you love the convenience of e-mail, you have to admit that the message format is pretty boring. Some brave souls have attempted to liven up their signature lines by creating a pattern that adds pizzazz. For example, instead of just plain "Dave," he might add:

```
DDDD          A       VVV   VVV    EEEEEE
DDDDD        AAA       VV    VV    EE
DD  DDD    A    A       VV VV      EEEEEE
DD  DDD   AAAAA          VVVV      EEEEEE
DDDDD    AA    AA         VVV      EE
DDDD    AA       AA        V       EEEEEE
```

But as bad as this looks, it gets even worse by the time the recipient's computer has worked its own particular brand of magic. For example, when Dave's e-mail message arrives, the signature has been scrambled, so it looks something like this:

```
   DDDD                     A             VVV   VEEEEEE
D   DD DD              AAA             VV    VV       EE
   D        DDDD    A    A                        VV       VV
EEE EEE
DD   DDAAAAAVVVV            EE  EEEE
      DD               DDD              AAAAVVV          EE
DD               DD                AA         AAVEEE EEE
```

The moral is: If you want to send dynamic e-mails that are colorful, well-designed, and graphically pleasing, use a service that ensures your readers will receive the same e-mail message you sent! This is particularly important if you are planning on using e-mail as a channel for promoting your business.

Services such as Constant Contact, iContact, or Benchmark allow you to design your own marketing e-mails in HTML format. This means that your e-mails will have the look of a Web page, but they show up in your recipients' inbox—not on their Web browser. If you are considering using e-mail for any kind of promotion, take into account the following advantages of using the services of an e-mail marketing program.

Templates. All of the popular e-mail marketing programs have ready-built templates you can use to format your message. The templates are many and varied, including association newsletters, real estate notices, travel promotions, and retail flyers. If you don't see anything that is an exact fit for your needs, you can create one from scratch or adapt any available design (most companies offer more than 300 templates) to be uniquely yours.

Each format has boxes where you can drag text, headers, photographs, spreadsheets, and so on, until you have created your message masterpiece. The HTML programming that translates your design into a language understood by e-mail clients all takes place in the background. The result is that what you see is what you get.

E-mail lists. Sending out online flyers, brochures, and notices requires keeping tabs on your e-mail address list, not just those that you send mail to, but also the responses you get back. E-mail marketing programs offer some great tools for making this job easy. Not only do they keep track of your mailing lists (you can keep different lists for different notices you send out), but they also track whether messages were opened, addresses that are no longer in use, duplicates, and those recipients who click the "unsubscribe" button and ask to be removed from the list.

Coaching and support. Constant Contact, iContact, and Benchmark all offer tons of support for the novice as well as the more seasoned online marketer. Some offer free support via e-mail or phone, and most are happy to put you on their mailing list to receive newsletters that contain useful tips and hints. For those of you who like a methodical approach, some providers provide step-by-step tutorials that remove any last remnants of doubt or tribulation.

Surveys. The latest development in e-mail marketing services is adding a survey feature to your message. It's always a good idea to get your audience involved in your message, and surveys are an effective way of doing this. The surveys are prewritten for customer satisfaction, new product testing, Website feedback, market research, and so on. Each template can be easily customized to fit your specific need, or, if you prefer, you can design your survey from the ground up. Results are tabulated in various different formats that can then be easily shared and exported.

> **No Free Lunch**
>
> None of the popular e-mail marketing services are free. However, there are differences between them, and it's a good idea to look at what each offers before buying a monthly subscription. Subscriptions run $10 to $30 per month for the basic package. Survey features and storage of media, such as photographs, will cost you a little extra.

50

Plan an E-Mail Marketing Newsletter

The upside of e-mail marketing is that it's a low-cost and convenient way for companies to communicate with their current customers and reach out to potential new ones. The downside of e-mail marketing is the fine line businesses walk between e-mails that customers have agreed to receive (opted in) and spam.

To increase the effectiveness of your e-mail marketing campaign, make the center of your strategy adding value to your target audience. Do this by providing them with pertinent and free advice. Online newsletters (e-newsletters) are one of the easiest and most effective ways of accomplishing this. Useful information always grabs attention, and increases the likelihood that your e-newsletter will be forwarded on to others not yet on your mailing list.

To create an interesting and dynamic e-newsletter, use a Web-based software service (such as iContact or Constant Contact) to turn your humble words and graphics into a snappy-looking HTML document. In other words, your e-mail looks like a Web page when viewed by the recipient. To help develop your newsletter strategy, take some time to think about what you want to accomplish.

What is the purpose of your newsletter?

- Is it primarily a way of staying in touch with your current customers?
- Will you use it to offer new products/services to existing clients?
- Do you want it to be passed on so that you can generate new customers?

Who is your audience?

- Do you want to reach senior managers, decision-makers, product users, lost clients, new clients?

What will make your audience want to read it?

- Will it offer up-to-date industry-specific information?
- Will it provide special offers on your products/services?
- What will it have that they cannot get elsewhere?

How frequently will you publish?

- Weekly, monthly, quarterly?

From where will your mailing list come?

- Will it be existing clients, identified potential clients, or every e-mail address you have on file?
- Will you purchase a mailing list?

What is the name of your e-newsletter?

- Does it communicate your purpose?
- Is it catchy and memorable?

What kind of image do you want to present?

- Formal, relaxed, fun, serious?
- Will it match your Website in style and design?

51

Send Out an E-Mail Marketing Newsletter

By planning and designing your e-newsletter, you greatly enhance its effectiveness. The next stage is dispatching the e-mail to its intended audience. However, before you click the *send* button, review the following points to make sure you have all your ducks in a row.

Is there a public holiday coming up? E-newsletters that are sent around holiday times often don't get read. People tend to focus only on the really pertinent items in their inbox at these times, and, consequently, your humble offering could be passed over or deleted.

Have you made a clear request of your audience? The more absorbing your newsletter, the more likely your audience is to want to take action. Your job is to make this as easy as possible. Does your e-newsletter make it obvious what you want readers to do? For example, if you are offering a special discount on your services, have you made it easy for the reader to click on a link, or respond by sending an e-mail to a specific address?

Hot Hint

Don't go overboard with links and special offers. Too many enticements can be confusing, and you end up with fewer responses.

Does your e-mail subject line read like spam? If it does, rethink it. Many people never get to the e-mail because the subject line is spammy. Choose a subject line that is compelling and likely to strike a chord with your audience.

Hot Hint

The top portion of your newsletter should grab your reader's attention. For example, if your e-mail is not fully opened and viewed in the preview pane, what will the reader see? Whatever it is, make it count by being interesting enough to make opening the document irresistible.

Is the boring stuff at the bottom? It should be. Don't use your prime real estate for unsubscribe links, disclaimers, or anything that is tedious, long-winded, or dreary. If readers need this information, they will find it.

Are you using too many typefaces? Keep it simple by using no more than two different fonts. Add emphasis and variety by using different font sizes, and bold and italic versions of the same font face. Keep exclamation points, dollar signs, and happy faces to a minimum.

Do you have a plan for unsubscribing people? All Web-based e-mail marketing software provides an automated unsubscribe process. Once the recipient clicks the *unsubscribe* button, his or her name is immediately removed from the mailing list. If you are using in-house programming for your mailings, make sure that unsubscribing is easy and fast.

What the Survey Says

In the E-Mail Marketing Metrics Report, March 2008 (available for download at *www.mailermailer.com/metrics*), the following tips, based on current research, are offered:

- Readers click more often on attractive, well-designed e-mails that offer useful and interesting information.
    - Give your readers a reason to click. Include a "Buy Now" button or a link to "Read the full story." Put just enough content to whet their appetite so they want more.
- To increase your open and click rates, try sending early in the week or on the weekends.
- Avoid words and symbols that spammers use, such as "FREE," "!!!," or "$," as these can hinder delivery.
- Some recipients will open your e-mail a couple of weeks or even longer after delivery. Make sure that your images, links, and landing pages remain accessible to them.

52

Get Good at Instant Messaging

If you've ever used your computer to have a typed conversation with colleagues or friends, then you've used instant messaging (IM). Services such as iChat, Skype, AIM, and MSN Messenger let you have an online talk-fest with anyone who has a computer, no matter where in the world they are—for free. Unlike e-mail, which can be one-sided due to delays in response, IM offers a real-time environment where you can see who is currently online and instigate a conversation immediately. Many IM programs also offer audio, video, and conferencing capabilities so that you can see and hear the other person(s). Add to this the ability to effortlessly exchange documents and photos, and you can see why instant messaging is the fastest-growing segment of the online communication market.

Because of its minimal cost, many Websites use instant messaging to provide customers with a fast and easy way to ask questions and get the kind of live information that was once delivered by phone. Clicking on a button quickly puts the customer in touch with an agent who responds with a typed "hello," and the conversation begins.

Using e-mail to communicate with customers can be challenging enough, but the rapid-fire nature of instant messaging adds some potential pitfalls that are unique to the medium. Here are the key issues to be aware of when using IM with customers.

Keep your sentences short. Long sentences keep the customer waiting (and require you to be a demon-fast typist), so keep them short. Mimic a spoken conversation by typing no more than

52

three sentences at a time, because this allows for an easy back-and-forth flow. If you're giving a long answer, be sure to break it up into short pieces for easier digestion and understanding.

Wait for a response. When you type and send your message, wait a few moments for customers to read and respond (if they are slow typists, this might take a while) before continuing on.

Explain wait times. If customers have to wait while you explore appropriate actions offline, they might think they have lost their connection when no typing appears on their screen. Avoid this by explaining what you are doing, why you are doing it, and how long you think it will take.

Avoid assumptions. If you are not certain what the customer is saying or asking, do not assume you know. People have different competency levels when it comes to expressing themselves in written words, so asking for clarification can save a ton of time down the road.

Use shorthand sparingly. Stay away from jargon, acronyms, and in-house abbreviations unless you are sure the customer is familiar with them. If you do not know, then play it safe by typing out the whole word or phrase. For example: Not everyone knows that CYL means "see you later."

Mirror back key points. When responding to a long and involved question, mirror the question back to the customer by paraphrasing your understanding of what he or she said. Wait for their response to see if you are on the money or need more clarification.

53

Study Your IM Shorthand

With instant messaging comes a whole new slew of shorthand terms that increase self-expression without typing-finger paralysis. Here are a few of the many in use.

2	To or Too
IMHO	In my humble opinion
4	For
LOL	Laughing out loud
4EVR	Forever
ROFL	Rolling on the floor laughing
Cuz	Because
K	Okay
NE1	Anyone
JK	Just kidding
EZ	Easy
JW	Just wondering
B4	Before
Luv	Love
BRB	Be right back

ILY	I love you
GTG	Got to go
WE	Weekend
CYL	See you later
TTFN	Ta-ta for now (goodbye)
BTW	By the way
TLLY	Totally
IDK	I don't know
W8	Wait
2nite	Tonight
2moro	Tomorrow
ZZZ	Tired or bored
OMG	Oh my God
XOXO	Hugs and kisses
U up	Are you up?
TMI	Too much information
BB4N	Bye-bye for now

54

E-Mail on a PDA

No matter how much you swoon over being able to dash out an e-mail while in the boardroom, on the bus, or under the weather, remember that e-mails sent with a handheld are not the same as those you send from your computer. Knowing the difference can make a big impression—even when using a tiny keyboard.

Get unattached from attachments. Unless absolutely necessary, omit adding attachments to your on-the-go PDA-sent e-mails. There's a good chance that they won't be readable at the recipient's end—they may not even show up. Send the attached document later, when back at your personal computer.

Give a heads-up. If you must send an attachment from a handheld, describe what you are sending so that the recipient understands your message even if the documents are missing or invisible.

Keep it brief. Not only will long messages damage your thumb joints, but they can also stimulate long-winded responses, which, in turn, lead to more thumb gymnastics on your end. Decide on the key points you want to make and focus on those.

Give your handheld credit. After your signature, add a line that says something like "Sent from my iPhone." This lets recipients know that you are on the move and limited in what you can send and receive.

Ask yes or no questions. Phrase your questions in such a way that respondents can easily respond with a one-word answer. For example, typing, "Can you meet me on Wednesday morning?" will get you a quick yes or no response. Writing, "I can meet with you almost any time this week. Let me know what works for you and I will see how it looks on my calendar" will require more time and typing on your end.

Small is no excuse for sloppy. You may be typing on a small keyboard while boarding the red-eye to Raleigh, but your message will probably be viewed on a large computer screen. Any spelling mistakes or punctuation problems will come across and can make you look less professional.

Think twice before responding. Is it really necessary to shoot off an e-mail while eating a Kosher frank with one hand and pulling your luggage cart with the other? Ask yourself if it makes more sense to respond when you get back to your desk or land at your destination.

Why We Love Our PDAs

A 2008 study of 6,500 professionals by Sheraton Hotels found that 62 percent of people surveyed love their PDA. Why? The same study found that 85 percent say that PDAs and cell phones allow them to spend more time out of the office, and 79 percent feel they can be just as productive outside of the office as inside.

55

Use POP and IMAP

POP and IMAP may sound like long-lost relatives of the Teletubbies, but they are, in fact, two different ways of receiving and sending e-mail messages. POP (post office protocol) is what you are using if you store your e-mails on your desktop computer and use programs such as Entourage, Outlook, or Eudora. IMAP (Internet message access protocol) is what you are using if you access and store your messages on a server that you access via the Web. Common IMAP programs are Hotmail, Gmail, and Yahoo Mail.

If you are considering setting up a new e-mail system, or are wondering about the advantages of one protocol over another, here is a cheat sheet that weighs up the pros and cons of each.

POP	IMAP
Primarily designed for accessing your e-mail from one computer.	You can access your e-mail messages from any computer with an Internet connection.
The whole message is downloaded.	It's faster to review new messages because only subject lines are initially downloaded.
Attachments are downloaded with the message and are stored on your computer.	Attachments are stored on the server and need to be downloaded. If you delete the message, you lose the attachment.
Storage is not a problem because messages are deleted from the server once downloaded.	Storage space limitation can be a hindrance.
Spam filtering is often inefficient.	Spam filtering is usually highly efficient.
Messages can be downloaded and then read when not connected to the Internet.	On some servers, messages can only be read when there's an online connection.
Autoresponders are often not available with POP e-mail programs.	Autoresponders are usually part of an IMAP setup.
POP requires paying a monthly server fee.	IMAP servers such as Gmail and Hotmail cost nothing.
If your computer crashes, you lose your messages.	Messages are safe on remote servers, which are backed up daily.
Message downloading is slow when using a slow connection.	Selective downloading saves time with slow connection speeds.
Copying your e-mails to another computer is cumbersome.	All messages are stored on the server, so there's never any need to transfer.
Migrating a message database to another e-mail program can be difficult or impossible.	Can be used with most e-mail programs, and a database is not necessary.

Making the Change?

IMAP protocol is rapidly becoming the protocol of choice for many people—especially those who need to access their messages from different locations. Also, IMAP dovetails nicely with other Web-based applications such as Google Docs, Zoho Writer, and Yahoo Calendar. If you're thinking of making the change from POP to IMAP, it's nice to know that most POP e-mail programs can easily be configured to access your online account.

56

Know When to Stop

Most businesspeople love the flexibility and convenience that e-mail and instant messaging have brought to their work life. Productivity no longer means being tethered to your desk—but it *does* mean being tethered electronically to your Blackberry, iPhone, or other PDA of choice. The upside of being wirelessly connected is always being in touch—at the airport, during lunch, and even on vacation! The downside is that you're *always* available, 24/7, 365 days a year—unless you know when to *stop* reading your e-mails!

A 2008 survey by the Pew Internet and American Life Project revealed that although 80 percent of wired workers believe that technology has improved their ability to do their job:

- 46 percent say that wireless technology has increased demands that they work more hours.
- 49 percent say it has increased the level of stress in their job, and makes it harder for them to disconnect from their work when they're at home evenings and weekends.

E-Mail In An Instant

With the lines between work, leisure, home, and office becoming ever more blurred, here are some ideas for reducing that "always on call" feeling.

Take tether breaks. Turn off your PDA or smartphone for 15 minutes during the day. Surprisingly, life won't come to a screeching halt. Use the time to focus, relax, read, or just do nothing.

Give your inbox a holiday. According to an AOL and Opinion Research Corporation survey, Americans are increasingly addicted to checking their e-mail, with 83 percent of survey respondents checking e-mail every day on vacation! If you *must* take a wired vacation, limit inbox activity to every two or three days.

> **Hot Hint**
>
> Leave your PDA at home, and if you must plug in, use an Internet café or the hotel computer.

Schedule weekend check-ins. If you need to check your e-mail during the weekend (do you really?), then schedule specific chunks of time to read and respond. For example, once on Saturday morning and once on Sunday evening. If you're worried about missing an important message, remember that most people will call your cell phone if there's an urgent matter.

Availability isn't obligation. Just because the telephone rings does not mean you are obligated to answer it. You have a choice—the same for e-mails and instant messages. Take charge by answering if you can, and when you want to.

The autoresponder is your friend. Don't limit your use of e-mail autoresponder to vacations and business trips. Instead, get creative, and if you want to take a few hours of "unplugged" time, harness the technology to let would-be e-mailers know you are out of reach and what they should do, or whom they should call in case of an emergency.

57

Don't Use E-Mail

Getting lulled into thinking that e-mail is the be-all, end-all of communication tools can get you into trouble. There are times when sending an e-mail is not the best way to communicate. Here are a few examples.

Time-sensitive subjects. Even though technology makes it possible for almost everyone to get their e-mail practically anyplace and anytime, don't assume that just because you send it, they will open it. If your matter is urgent or highly time-sensitive, contact the other person by phone as well.

Employee counseling. Coaching and counseling can be delicate conversations to negotiate, because body language and tone of voice play a key part in showing appreciation and understanding of the other person's feelings. Whenever possible, coaching and counseling should be done face-to-face or over the telephone—not via e-mail.

Confidential information. E-mail is *never* private. Use fax, face-to-face communication, or the telephone when dealing with any of the following.

- Compensation and salary numbers.
- Account numbers.
- Medical reports.
- Social Security numbers.
- Financial details of any kind.

Inflammatory topics. Trying to respond to an e-mail that contains inflammatory information, such as a rumor that the boss is being fired, the company taken over, or yearly bonuses cut, will only add fuel to the fire. E-mails can be misinterpreted and rumors spread online like wildfire. If the topic is hot, it's best doused with an in-person response.

Important announcements. When something big is happening at work, people want information. Their need to ask questions, allay their fears or concerns, and discuss the news with others is paramount. Instead of announcing events that have a big impact on staff online (such as using e-mail to notify employees that the company is being taken over), deliver these messages in person through all-hands or small group meetings.

Emotional issues. When dealing with someone who is having a strong emotional reaction (such as conflict with a coworker), e-mail simply doesn't work. Even if you are trying to say all the right things in a message, its impersonal nature can come across as uncaring. In situations in which the other person is upset, sad, or angry, deal with him or her face-to-face or on the phone.

Complex information. Presenting information that requires a long description and/or has many twists and turns via e-mail is a recipe for misunderstanding. For the dissemination and discussion of complex information, an in-person meeting works best. Others can ask questions, double-check their understanding of a situation, and freely discuss the finer points of the information being presented.

When you're upset. If you write an e-mail when you are angry or upset, you may later regret what you said in the heat of the moment. Remember, you can't retrieve a message once you've hit the *send* button. So give yourself a chance to cool down before communicating.

58

Manage Your Files

Not only is it important to design a filing system for your inbox that reflects the way you work, but it's equally important to keep track of all the default folders that come as part and parcel of your e-mail program. Namely: Drafts, Sent, Spam, and Trash.

The Drafts folder is primarily designed to store messages that you have written but not completed. If, after composing an e-mail, you close the message window (rather than the normal procedure of hitting *send*), you are asked if you would like to save a draft of the file. If you do, it is sent to the Drafts folder.

Drafts folders are also useful for storing e-mail templates (such as form letters, product instructions, and directions), or any message you send repeatedly and requires minimal customization. After preparing the original message to use as a template, save it to the Drafts folder. The next time you need to send the information, open the saved e-mail, copy the contents, and paste it into a new message window ready for sending.

Beware: Drafts folders can get clogged up with incomplete e-mails that were never sent (including those that you were in the middle of when your system crashed), and outdated templates that you no longer use. To stay organized, go through your Drafts file once every three months and delete any messages you no longer need or use.

The Sent folder can be used in different ways depending on how you set your e-mail program's preferences. Many people automatically save every message they send so that they always have a complete record of all outgoing e-mails. Although this is a convenient method, it does take up room on your hard drive, especially if you send a lot of big attachments such as photos, music, or design files.

Most programs offer you a choice about when to delete sent messages: a day, a week, a month, or never. Because the first three options delete *all* messages indiscriminately, many people choose the "never" option and then go through their Sent folder every week or so and remove all the messages they no longer need.

Alternatively, you can switch off the auto-saving feature, and then CC yourself on any outgoing message that you feel it's important to save. When the message arrives in your inbox, file it in the appropriate folder.

The Spam folder holds all the junk mail that never makes its way to your inbox. It has an auto-delete feature that you can control through the program's preferences pane; usually one day, one week, and one month—or never. Because some real messages can get caught in the Spam trap, check your junk mail folder once a day just to stay on top of any mislabeled strays. Setting your auto-delete feature to once a week allows enough time to conduct a regular check. If you find e-mails that are not spam, drag them to your inbox or other relevant folder.

Unlike Spam, the Trash folder holds messages before they are permanently deleted, and as such can offer you a second chance at recovery, if you mistakenly ditch a message that you discover you need. For this reason it's a good idea to have your Trash folder keep its contents for a week or so, rather than going for the "delete when I quit the program" option. Better safe than sorry.

Archiving

To minimize wasted computer space—especially if you have mucho messages—consider archiving your mailboxes. Archiving compresses your e-mails so that they no longer reside within your e-mail program, but as a separate file that takes up very little room. The downside is that the compressed formatting makes them a little harder to read—a small cost for an efficient and easy way of backing up your messages.

59

Set Up Your Filing System

One big key to e-mail efficiency is knowing how to file messages so that they are easy to retrieve when you need them. All e-mail programs offer filing options that allow you to set up your storage system in a way that reflects the way you work—and possibly the way you already have your paper files organized. Here are a few main options.

File by client name. If your work is account-based, with lots of different clients, it makes sense to set up a folder for each customer. For example:

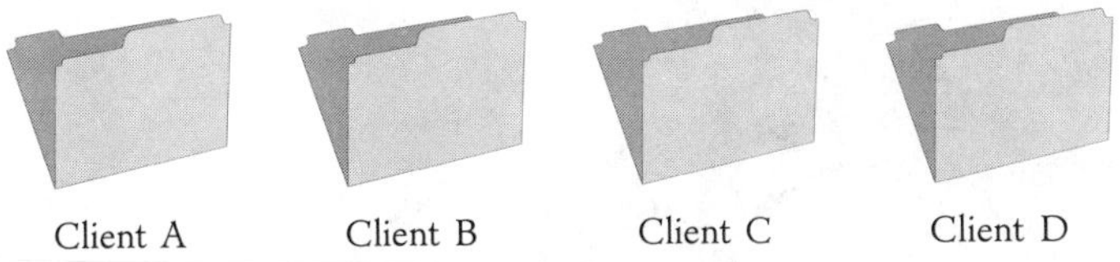

However, if you have several hundred clients to keep tabs on (no pun intended), create general folders that divide the clients into broader categories. For example:

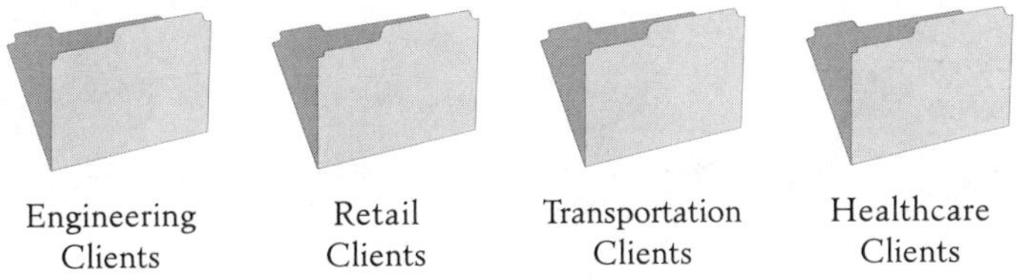

Alternatively, create general alphabetized folders such as:

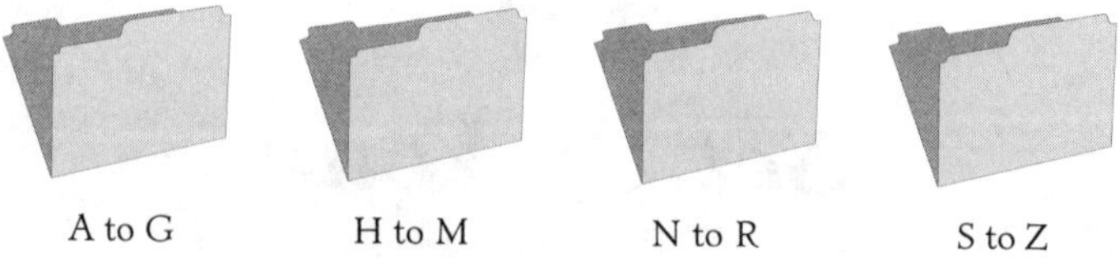

Once you have your main folders set up, you can create subfolders for each client and place their subfolders within the appropriate general folder. For example: If you are using an alphabet system, Dehydrate Water Exporters, Inc., would go in file A to G. If you are using the client category system, all engineering clients are placed in subfolders within the engineering folder:

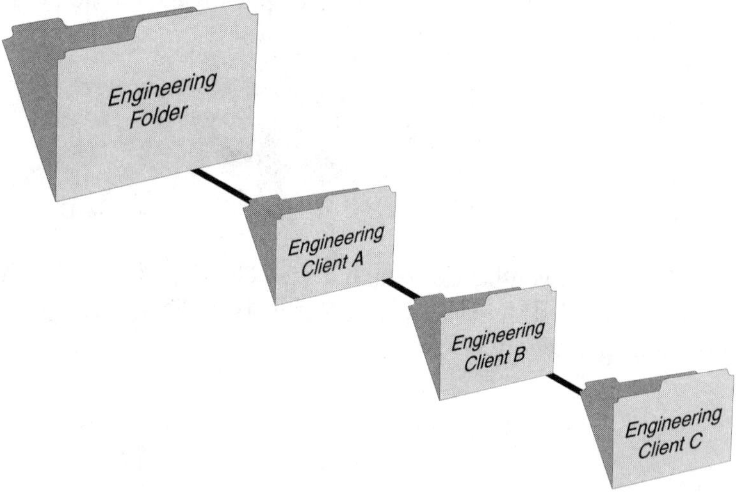

59

File by product. If your work has more to do with products and services than clients, make general folders for all the main categories you deal with. For example:

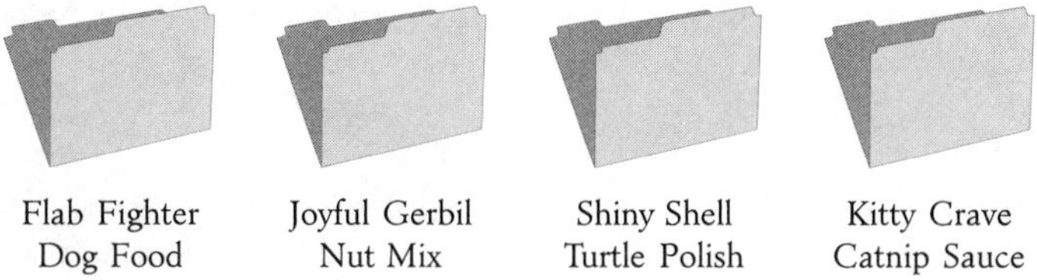

Within these folders place all related topics within subfolders. For example:

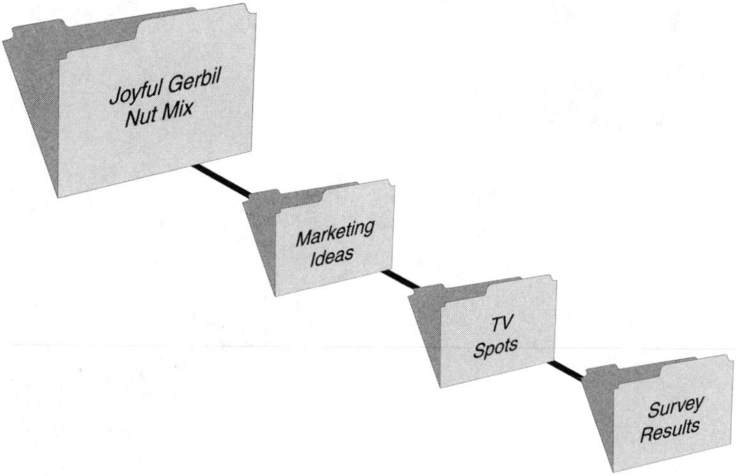

File by project. Some people prefer a project-based filing system in which folders are created for each of the major projects you are working on. For example:

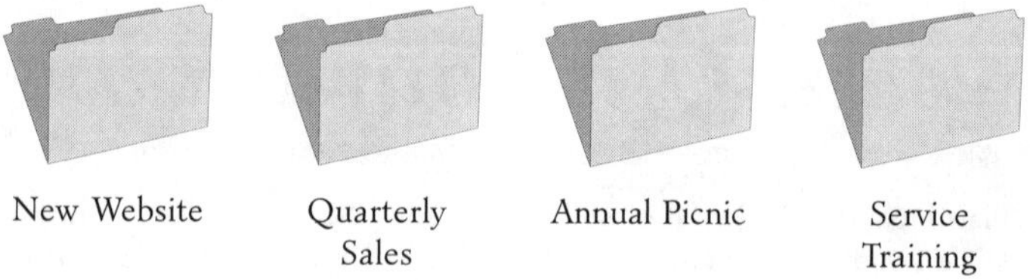

Within each folder, subfolders can be created to store messages that relate to one area of the project. For example:

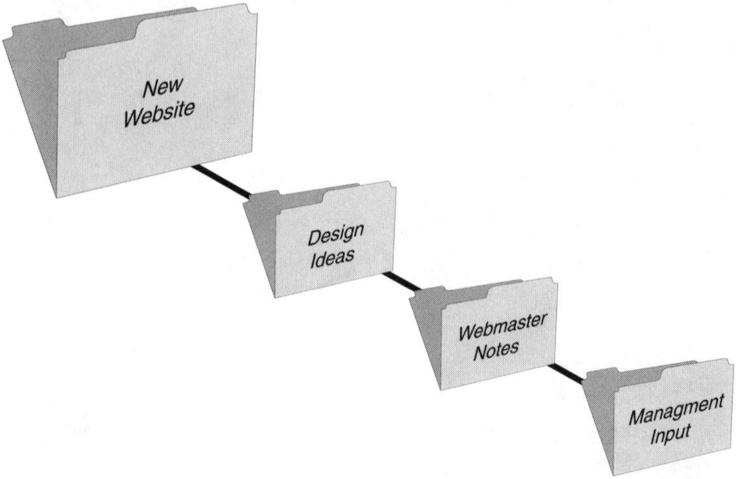

Hot Hint: Automated Filing

Microsoft Outlook, Entourage, and Apple Mail have features for automatically assigning e-mails—from specific senders, or about certain subjects—to pre-assigned folders. E-mails then show up in your main inbox list, but are also filed under their specified topic.

60

Zero Out Your Inbox

Without doubt, a crisis of e-mail overload is wreaking havoc with our time, attention, productivity, and even peace of mind! Most people don't have a good system in place for processing incoming messages quickly and easily. Instead, messages languish in the inbox, gathering dust and waiting to be dealt with. One way to keep a rein on inbox insanity is to go for a goal of zeroing out your inbox every day by making a definite decision about what to do with each incoming e-mail.

Borrow a tip from the book *Time Management In An Instant*, and zero out your inbox with the four D system.

Do. Some items that pop up in your inbox require or inspire you to take immediate action. If the message you see can be handled easily and quickly (say within five minutes), do it now. Once done, delete the item or move it to the appropriate folder for storage. If the item can't be completed easily, move it to a folder for items to be done, or flag it for completion at some point during the day. At the end of the day, all the flagged items that are unfinished should be moved to the "to be done" folder.

Delete. If an e-mail sits in your inbox waiting to be worked on for days, weeks, or even months, you may be putting off the completion of the item for several reasons, including: It is too big to handle as is and needs to be broken down into bite-size chunks; the item is not clearly defined enough for you to take action on; or it is something you don't really, want, need, or intend to do. If this last reason fits, there is no shame in hitting the *delete* button and saying so long to that message muddling up your inbox.

Hot Hint

In the face of too much to do, with too little time and too few resources, it's easy to panic and abandon ship on e-mails that in the end would have been worthwhile to pursue. Before dumping any item of significance or impact, reflect on your priorities and how important its getting done is for your overall goals and objectives.

Delegate. The fact that you received the e-mail message does not mean you have to be the one to execute it. A great strategy for clearing out your inbox is to transfer it to someone else's. Considerations, of course, need to be given to the other person's availability, ability, and willingness, but the option of passing on a piece of the work to someone else is a real one. Ask yourself if you really need to be the one to handle an item.

Defer. Many items in your inbox are good ideas you would like to follow up on—just not now. Instead of letting the someday item sit in your active inbox file, create a "to do," "pending," or "someday" folder where you can keep tabs on messages you may want to take action on at some point in the future.

By reflecting on your priorities, goals, and commitments you can more easily determine which bits and pieces don't require action today, and can be put off until tomorrow. The key is to immediately clear the item out of your inbox and move it to another file where you can easily retrieve it when you are ready to work on it.

Ask yourself, is it essential or important that this be done today, or can it wait? Would there be any serious negative consequences if I delayed doing this item?

Exercise

Five Minutes to a Cleaner Inbox

Open your e-mail inbox and then set your watch, alarm clock, computer, or iPhone on a five-minute timer. Now, starting from the top (the latest e-mail), go through and see how many items you can get completed and moved out of your mailbox using the four D's: Do, Delete, Delegate, or Defer.

Conclusion

We are at a turning point in business today. Tools such as e-mail, instant messaging, and online chat have become an integral part of our everyday workplace. This influx of technology into almost every facet of business life has created a streamlined workplace that often collides with our increased need for human contact.

Throughout the past years we have interviewed more than 25,000 businesspeople in our seminars and presentations, asking them, "What's the single biggest challenge you face in today's business environment?" Time and again we hear variations on the same theme: "How do we stay in touch and connected to each other, in a high-tech world?"

Keeping in touch via e-mail requires remembering that the traditional workplace values of relationship, courtesy, and etiquette are more relevant than ever in a world where a passion for technology—without a passion for substance—seems rampant.

We sincerely hope that *E-Mail In An Instant* has helped you discover the path to maintaining and enriching your online relationships, and that this book will find a permanent home on your business bookshelf.

Index

A

acronyms, using, 95
action, detailed, 35-36
announcements, important, 144
anti-phishing software, 109
apostrophes, correct usage of, 72-74
archiving, benefits of, 96
assumptions, avoiding, 135
attachment options, considering, 62-63
attachments, opening, 64-65
autoresponder, benefits of using an, 96

B

BCC, rules of, 60-62
body language, interpreting, 19
brainstorming, 120
business communication, 17

C

capital letters, overusing, 95
capitalizing, importance of, 79-81
CCing,
  rules of, 58-60
  unnecessary, 17
client name, filing by, 147
commas, correct usage of, 74-76
communication, business, 17
confidential information, 143
conjunctions, eliminating, 66
contractions, saving time with, 77-79
conversation, face-to-face, 51
conversations, telephone, 51
counseling, employee, 143
cultural differences, considering, 113-116

D

data mining, 61
dialogue, engaging in, 20
discussion, inviting, 46
distribution lists, 97-98

E

emoticons,
  obscure, 103-105
  using, 95
emotional issues, 144
employee counseling, 143
etiquette mistakes, 17
expressive style, engaging the, 41

F

face-to-face conversation, 51
feedback, inviting, 46
files, managing your, 145
filing system, setting up your, 147-150
filters, negative, 102-103
firewalls, 98
flame, definition of a, 99-101
formal greetings, 50
formal neutral language, 31-33

G

greetings, formal, 50

H

homophones, getting hung up on, 89-92

I

IMAP, using, 139-141
inbox, zero out your, 151
individuals, results-oriented, 44
inflammatory topics, 143
information,
  complex, 144
  confidential, 143
instant messaging, 134-135
IP address, 98
issues, emotional, 144

J

jargon, understanding, 96-99

K

key words, mirroring, 28-31

M

marketing newsletter,
  planning a, 129-131
  sending out a, 131-133
marketing service, finding a, 126-129
message tone, 38
mining, data, 61
misspelled words, mastering, 83-87
mistakes, e-mail, 92
modality, sensory, 31

N

negative filters, 102-103
neutral language, formal, 31-33
newsletter, marketing, 129-131
newsletters, online, 129
nice and easy style, 44
no,
  hard, 39
  learning to say, 39-40

P

paragraph, least important, 23
paragraphs,
  prioritizing, 22-23
  using short, 18
PDA, communicating on a, 137-139
phishing, avoiding, 108-110
phone, knowing when to use your, 111
policy,
  creating a, 116-117
  writing an e-mail, 117-119
POP, using, 139-141
privacy,
  protecting, 61
  respecting, 17
problem causes,
  brainstorming, 120-121
  evaluating, 122-123
problem solutions,
  brainstorming, 123-124
problem-solving style, 48-50
product, filing by, 149
punctuation, poor, 94

R

requests,
  making effective, 35-37
  unclear, 94
responses, getting, 35
responsible rant, setting up a, 112-113
results-oriented individuals, 44

S

salutation, starting with a, 50-52
security blunders, 110
security, e-mail, 110-112
sensory
  language, discovering the secret of, 25-28
  modality, 31
  style, words for, 26
sentence length, varying your, 68-69
sentence style, choosing your, 70-72
sentences,
  interrogative, 71
  hortening your, 65-67
stream-of-consciousness, 71
serious tone, projecting a, 48
server, using a, 63
shorthand, studying your, 136-137
signing off, rules for, 55-58
software, anti-phishing, 109
spam,
  avoiding, 53
  sorting through, 106-107
spelling, sharpening your, 87-89
straight-shooter style, 44
stress, causing, 61
style,
  nice and easy, 44
  problem-solving, 48-50
  straight-shooter, 44
subject line,
  crafting a, 52-55
  typical, 19
subject lines, good, 18-19
surveys, benefits of, 128-129

T

telephone conversations, 51
templates, building, 127
time frame, requesting a specific, 36

time-sensitive subjects, 143
tone,
  message, 38
  serious, 48
  unprofessional, 95
topics, inflammatory, 143
transitions,
  importance of, 82-83
  long sentences with, 66
typefaces, using too many, 132

U

understanding, gaining mutual, 36-37

V

verbs, power, 33-35

W

weekend check-ins, scheduling, 142
writing, effective, 38

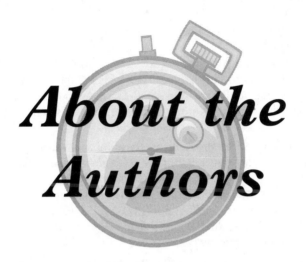

About the Authors

Keith Bailey and **Karen Leland** are cofounders of Sterling Consulting Group (*www.scgtraining.com*), an international management consulting firm specializing in maximizing results through the people side of business. In business for 25 years, they have worked with more than 150,000 executives, managers, and front-line staff from a wide variety of industries including retail, transportation, hospitality, high-tech, banking, and consumer goods.

Their consulting work in corporations and public speaking engagements has taken them throughout North America, Southeast Asia, Africa, and Europe. Their clients have included such companies as AT&T, American Express, Apple Computer, Avis Rent-A-Car, Bank of America, Bristol-Myers Squibb, the British Government, DuPont, SC Johnson Wax, Lufthansa German Airlines, Microsoft, and Oracle, to name a few.

In addition to their consulting work, Karen and Keith are sought-after experts by the media. They have been interviewed by dozens of newspapers, magazines, and television and radio stations, including: The Associated Press International, *Time*, *Fortune*, *Newsweek*, *The New York Times*, *Entrepreneur Magazine*, *Ladies Home Journal*, *Self Magazine*, *Fitness Magazine*, CNN, *The Today Show*, and Oprah.

They are sought-after speakers and have presented for groups such as the Young Presidents Organization, the Society of Association Executives, the Society of Consumer Affairs, and the Direct Marketing Association.

Karen and Keith are the authors of five books, including three editions of the bestselling *Customer Service For Dummies* (Wiley Publishing) that has sold more than 250,000 copies and been translated into Spanish, German, Korean, Chinese, and Polish, among other languages.

In addition, Karen and Keith are the authors of *Watercolor Wisdom: How Smart People Prosper in the Face of Conflict, Pressure and Change* (New Harbinger, 2006), *Customer Service In An Instant: 60 Ways to Win Customers and Keep Them Coming Back* (Career Press, 2008), *Time Management In An Instant: 60 Ways to Make the Most of Your Day* (Career Press, 2008), and *Public Speaking In An Instant: 60 Ways to Stand Up and Be Heard* (Career Press, 2009).

On the Web, Karen Leland is national work-life columnist for examiner.com. Visit her posts at *www.examiner.com/x-728-Work-Life-Balance-Examiner.*

About Sterling Consulting Group

Sterling Consulting Group offers a variety of training programs, consulting, and keynote speeches. To learn more about our on-site training programs, or to book Karen or Keith to speak at your next event, please visit the Website at *www.scgtraining.com.* For any additional questions or to schedule an interview, contact Keith Bailey or Karen Leland at:

Sterling Consulting Group
3030 Bridgeway #220
Sausalito, CA 94965
(415) 331-5200
info@scgtraining.com
www.scgtraining.com